Praise for *No Excuses*

"If you are looking for more joy and meaning in your life (and who isn't?) then you must read this book."
—**Hernando de Soto**, founder of the Institute for Liberty & Democracy, winner of the Milton Friedman Prize

"A compelling story and a tribute to the power of the human spirit to ever renew itself."
—**John Kitzhaber**, MD, Governor of Oregon

"David Neenan reminds us that it's how we learn from our mistakes that makes us who we are—happy or miserable."
—**Alan K. Simpson**, US Senator, Wyoming (retired)

"This book is so meaningful I read it twice."
—**John Hill**, venture capitalist, Hyde Park Capital Partners

"A very sweet tale, full of wisdom."
—**Fred Kofman**, author of Conscious Business

"David Neenan shows us how to tackle our challenges head on—No Excuses is a must-read for anyone who wants to gain insight into enjoying the journey."
—**Sonny Lubick**, former head football coach, Colorado State University

NO EXCUSES

*Take Responsibility
for Your Own Success*

DAVID NEENAN
with ERIC LUCAS

NEW YORK

NO EXCUSES

Take Responsibility for Your Own Success

DAVID NEENAN
with ERIC LUCAS

ISBN 978-1-61448-027-3 Paperback
ISBN 978-1-61448-028-0 ePub Version
Library of Congress Control Number: 2011928013

Published by:
MORGAN JAMES PUBLISHING
The Entrepreneurial Publisher
5 Penn Plaza, 23rd Floor
New York City, New York 10001
(212) 655-5470 Office
(516) 908-4496 Fax
www.MorganJamesPublishing.com

Cover Design by:
Rachel Lopez
rachel@r2cdesign.com

Interior Design by:
Bonnie Bushman
bbushman@bresnan.net

In an effort to support local communities, raise awareness and funds, Morgan James Publishing donates one percent of all book sales for the life of each book to Habitat for Humanity. Get involved today, visit
www.HelpHabitatForHumanity.org.

Table of Contents

Foreword

Moscow, Russia, is ten hours ahead of Fort Collins, Colorado. So when the phone rang in the Fort Collins home of David and Sharon Neenan at 2:00 AM it was noon in Moscow.

"You better take this call," was Sharon's assessment as she grasped the significance of the middle-of-the-night interruption. David complied.

In perfect English the man from Moscow introduced himself as Igor, a name as common as Peter is in the United States. Igor explained that he had taken David's *Business & You* course two years prior (1992) in Moscow, not long after the Soviet Union had collapsed and Russians were seeking expanded knowledge of the world outside the Iron Curtain. David racked his brain to recall exactly who Igor was, and came up with a face he believed went with the name.

David asked, "So what have you been doing these past two years?"

"I have been studying English," was Igor's prompt reply.

"Why would you do that?" was David's next question.

"So I could call and thank you in English for changing my life," was the response.

If someone told you that the basic roadmap for a meaningful life is available in a book of less than 200 pages, would you read it? That is what *No Excuses* offers.

On one level, *No Excuses* is about David's journey through a life of personal responsibility. On another level this book is about much more than David's "story." It is not about asking the reader to be like David. Rather, the personal and business stories are just examples of how David's "no excuses" approach surfaces certain "Generalized Success Principles." His personal examples are simply examples for the reader to understand David's path to experiencing a meaningful life.

While some of David's success principles may seem simple, they are not simplistic. The sheer weight and connectivity of his stories and ideas make the book coalesce brilliantly. It is this amalgamation of illustrative examples and corollary principles that make this a profound book.

I'm convinced the more you absorb this modest book (please do read it all!) the greater the probability you will have a meaningful life. It's your decision whether to invest your time and energy in doing this. As Albert Camus once said, "Life is the sum of all your choices."

Marshall Thurber, Partner
The Global Evolutionary Network
marshall@globalevolutionary.com
www.globalevolutionary.com

Don't Be a Sea Squirt

Don't wait for the last judgment—it takes place every day.—
Albert Camus

Life begins as a glorious adventure for sea squirts—a large
and numerous class of ocean creatures known as tunicates. In the
larval stage, they float free, roaming underwater tides and currents
like globe-trotting teenagers, wending their way wherever fate
takes them while seeing the world and encountering new creatures,
terrains, and experiences. They are seafaring adventurers.

But as maturity sets in, tunicates find a handy rock, send out a
holdfast, and cement themselves to a spot where they will spend
the rest of their lives sucking up whatever comes their way. They
cover themselves with stiff, unyielding membranes compared
to "tunics," thus the biological name, and stay put. Forever. No
longer needing to move, they begin their existence as adults by
digesting their own cerebral ganglion.

That's their brain.

Having settled down from youthful adventure, they turn their
thinking apparatus into dinner.

I see this a lot. Far too many human beings live like sea squirts—the difference being that most people don't manage to digest their entire brain matter—while spending decades leading the lives of quiet desperation that Thoreau lamented. Stuck fast in one spot, or one bad relationship, or one colorless job, or a powerful addiction, these human tunicates build thick membranes that shield them from both challenge and accomplishment. They make mental and spiritual holdfasts that pin them down, and they even create belief systems that declare this stagnation the best possible choice. Miserable, they seek the false comfort of deceit or despair or drugs or alcohol and spread their pain to their families, partners, communities, and sometimes whole countries. They excuse this behavior with explanations that the average sea squirt would endorse—fear, inevitability, biological destiny, and the list goes on.

I could not have become one of these people.

Family circumstances brought me early challenges that catalyzed the life of action, learning, and exploration I have enjoyed. My very nature guided my choices—but they were choices, and that's the message of this book.

What adult sea squirts do is called "filter feeding." Whatever the world sends you, down your gullet it goes—right away. That's called instant gratification; I'll return to that concept later in this book. If you are a sea squirt, you simply swallow what comes your way on the spot, suck out a little nourishment, and what's left emerges from the other end like a sewage plant. But we are not sea squirts, and how we conduct our lives is our choice.

The many choices I have made—some good, some bad— form the fabric of the stories in this book. They tell how I discovered my character and purpose in life; met and married my partner, Sharon; founded a thriving construction company; and struggled through challenges ranging from potential bankruptcy to spiritual breakdown.

Many of these life stories also compose portions of the personal growth workshops I have taught around the world for twenty-five years under the title "Business and You." From China to my hometown of Fort Collins, Colorado, thousands of people have taken this course. Such people include my coauthor, Eric Lucas. Eric and I met when I was president of the school board in Fort Collins, and he was a reporter at the local newspaper.

Please keep in mind that the stories in this book can change your life only if you get out there and take action. Only in action are we truly alive; no, sitting still and swallowing whatever shows up in your mouth isn't "action." Each story illustrates how I learned something, but everything I've learned is the result of action I've taken. Reading these stories doesn't equal learning.

It's your choice—stay put and filter-feed, or let go of your holdfast and get going. Give love, learn as much as you can, honor your family and friends, and help improve the beautiful world we share.

And what if sea squirts someday did manage to abandon their rocks, their shells, their stagnant lives, and set sail on the ocean as adventurous adults? Luckily, as human beings we already have the choice to find that out, every single day.

Beginnings: It's time to grow up

When we are no longer able to change a situation, we are challenged to change ourselves. —Viktor Frankl

I was eleven years old the day the front doorbell rang and my family's fortunes changed forever.

It was an early summer Saturday, a fair day that promised a warm enough afternoon for swimming, or just tumbling around outdoors in shorts. My mom was bustling through our Columbia, Missouri, house picking up the debris my seven siblings and I had scattered around. My dad was away in St. Louis at a statewide meeting of greengrocers. I was headed outside to play with friends down the street—kick the can, maybe, or home run derby.

This was 1954, and the fifties were halcyon times in America; postwar peace and prosperity brought a sense of infinite potential. My dad left his unfulfilling job as a Nabisco route driver to take over a produce stand out on the main highway, and things seemed to be going well. His lifelong dream to have his own business was becoming reality.

My brother Dan and I would often go out to the Highway Fruit Market on Saturday mornings and unload trucks full of watermelons, or help stack corn in display bins. Columbia was a great place to grow up, a quiet college town of tree-lined streets in the middle of rolling Missouri countryside. When I had spare time in the summer, we'd go fishing for perch and swimming in old quarries, or hop on a freight train to McBain and go riding.

That Saturday morning, though, I overheard snatches of adult conversation at the front door that carried an ugly undertone. My mom talked a few minutes with our visitor, then came back into the living room with an envelope in her hand. She was crying.

"Mom, what's wrong?" I asked.

"David, your dad and I are being sued. We're going to lose our store," she explained.

The visitor was an attorney, infamous in Columbia as a hardcore shark, and he'd handed my mother a lawsuit notice. The contract under which my dad had taken over the produce store required that its books be kept by a professional outside accountant; instead, to save money he'd had my mother do the bookkeeping. The lawsuit claimed breach of contract and demanded return of title to the fruit stand.

"Why did he come today? A Saturday, with Dad out of town?" I asked.

"He said they considered the element of surprise important," my distraught mother replied, barely able to talk.

And so I was introduced to the harsher side of life. Our family had no money to fight the lawsuit; the attorney my dad consulted said we had no choice but to hand the store back to its previous owner. Dad had invested $10,000, mostly borrowed, and turned a losing proposition into a thriving enterprise. He lost every penny, and the once-and-future owner, an already wealthy man, regained a valuable property that he then sold to someone else for a profit. Dad went back to his job as a Nabisco rack jobber (route salesman), and losing his store was the pivotal point at which he surrendered his ambitions in life and lost himself in drinking and despair.

That Saturday was my first existential moment, the first occasion when the vast potential of life—for good or ill—burst upon my consciousness. Existentialism is the term applied to a broad area of twentieth-century philosophy whose adherents believe the individual is the source of all human meaning, that our choices derive from our own values, not those imposed from outside.

Good and evil, joy and fear—these are facts of existence, and rather than maunder about their origins, existentialists simply accept them and carve out their own lives. We are not sea squirts. We are born with free will and are accountable for the choices we make in the face of these facts of existence. That's my interpretation of the existential challenge to us, the living. Since these challenges at first seem negative and derive from troubling events, the common picture of existentialism is that it's a nihilistic, cynical view of life. But I'd have to disagree. Taking responsibility for your life is both courageous and liberating. Facing life's challenges leads not toward darkness, but toward the light.

I recall being filled with rage when I saw my mother so badly hurt. It was despicable to spring such a surprise on a kind and decent woman on a quiet weekend morning. I knew that. And I realized that our meager circumstances meant we simply had to tuck our heads down and take it.

At the same time, a glimmer of another much different realization germinated in me. I didn't have to surrender, even if my dad chose to.

The notion of choice is one of the fulcrums of existential philosophy, not to mention life itself. Though I call that Saturday surprise an existential moment, I had no concept of such a thing at age eleven. I did know a few things, though. The attorney who came to our door did not have to act as he did. He chose his course. And my dad didn't have to choose my mother to keep the books; he made a bad choice.

My anger told me that I had the capacity to experience deep passion about life—a profound gift—and that within me burned an indomitable fire to fight for what I feel is necessary and worthy in life.

As a result, I recognized that I could choose what to do. Remember the psychological studies from the nineties that demonstrated that boys have innate drives to strike and throw things? I was a young boy; I knew how to get in trouble, and I often did so over the next decade.

But I also knew how to work. I'd been mowing lawns, selling newspapers, and washing cars since I was eight. And I'd been helping my dad at the fruit stand. I got a firsthand look at how running a business could be fun and rewarding. I devoted a lot of time and energy to working as I grew up, learning to provide for myself and those I love.

I knew my family was just about the most important thing in life. I hated seeing my mom cry. I hated seeing my dad give up.

When you're young, you have an infinite amount of time and energy to experiment on various ways of being, so for quite a while I pursued several simultaneously. I was a half-baked juvenile delinquent: I got caught joyriding in a "borrowed" car, was arrested for malicious mischief, and got off only because my partner in crime (vandalism) was the son of the business school dean. James Dean, with his cigarette, slouch, and sneer, was my idol. My first stab at a college education fizzled. A teacher asked me, "Since when have you settled for mediocrity?" A realization dawned. "All my life," I replied, not that I changed direction at that instant.

But I tasted the sweet savor of self-won success, too. A caring high school principal insisted I take a key role in a student production of *Finian's Rainbow,* and I adored the sound of applause—applause for me, the bad boy who'd been caught joyriding. As a teenager, I worked for the local paper, the *Columbia Missourian*, and was promoted several times to more responsible positions.

These events and the choices I made set the stage for the rest of my life. I believe fervently that we all have the power to choose our destiny, despite what comes our way. At age eleven, I had been powerless to fend off the disaster that struck my dad's business, but I was not powerless to live my own life. Subconsciously, at least, I must have wondered why my dad set aside his dreams in the face of one failure. It was a major loss, to be sure, but failure is defeat only if you call it defeat.

Most lives have several fulcrum points. They often seem to arrive in the form of a crisis, and these are the times when we choose whom to be. This is the crux of the existential dilemma: Life presents opportunities for one of three responses—to choose active participation, no matter the circumstances; to surrender to circumstances and adopt bitter resignation; or to just hide within the vague discontent and anxiety that are the hallmarks of modern life.

The last two choices are the doorways to futility and unhappiness. Bitter resignation predetermines both the outlook and the outcome of a life. Choosing to hide—putting down a holdfast and staying put for a lifetime—is a passive-aggressive response to the universe: *I submit to victimhood.* Choosing action is a decision made in passion, in heartfelt commitment to the experience and wonder of life. It's the better choice by far, but it's not an easy path.

I'm conscious of this only in retrospect, though, even as a boy, I believe I had a subconscious understanding of the need for passionate action. Live first, then philosophize—so urged Marcus Aurelius. My life has been devoted to universal human aspirations such as creating financial security for my family, learning the principles of achievement and growth, working and living with other people in honor and love. I've sought meaning and joy in life, and have discovered it in the simplest places: work, family, and helping to make a better world.

That early experience was just one of many pivotal moments, but it was crucial. My mother's tears were not in vain.

Chapter 2

Go For It: The only failure
is not to participate

*Only those who will risk going too far can possibly find out
how far one can go.* —T. S. Eliot

*Most men lead lives of quiet desperation and go to the grave
with their song still in them.* —Henry Thoreau

My lawyers said sue.

Accountants urged me to file for bankruptcy.

Worst of all, I felt the prickles of despair for the first time in
my life.

More than twenty years after the painful day my dad lost his
produce store, I faced a similar but even bigger crisis. I'd bought
and built up a commercial construction company in Fort Collins,
Colorado, and I named it after my dad. I had a home and family I
loved. I was part of a growing, progressive community. A business
crisis threatened it all.

I smoked more than a pack of cigarettes a day. I slept poorly at
night. I had just experienced a devastating injury on the racquetball
court that cost a body part near and dear to all men.

The Neenan Company was losing a huge amount—$670,000—on a project in Casper, Wyoming. Should I sue? File bankruptcy?

It was an ugly situation.

A 1976 photo taken of me then shows a cocky young businessman, sitting up in bed "recovering" from the racquetball injury, phone to my ear, cigarette in hand, the *Wall Street Journal* by my side. It's not a pretty picture. I still have it, photographic documentation of some of the bad choices I've made.

The whole experience—I call it the "Casper disaster"—was one more among the turning points of my life. It presented huge challenges that forced me to choose not just specific responses, but an overall philosophy. Would I duck and run? Or would I go for it? Yes, another existential moment.

The first choice, duck and run, is practically endemic. Each year more than two million Americans file for bankruptcy. Lawsuits number in the millions, including many filed by people who sue over personal choices they have made, such as smoking. Some of these attempts to shift responsibility are desperate decisions representing the last resort for people; but, justified or not, shifting responsibility does not create strength and understanding.

Caution and avoidance pervade virtually all of life, even sports. It's gospel in American football that the sensible choice on fourth down is to punt the ball away; coaches who go for it and try to make the first down, are considered daring at best, if not outright crazy. But then, why are there four downs in the first place? A University of California, Berkeley, professor, who applied economics models to football, found that punting is often a poor choice. David Romer analyzed more than twenty thousand National Football League plays and found that "going for it" on fourth down was a better decision more than half the time. He theorized that coaches know that, but choose safety, because the consequences of taking the risk and failing—such as getting fired—are perceived to be much worse.

Safety certainly sounded like a rational choice in my situation. If I sued or claimed bankruptcy, perhaps the business would survive. I had three young daughters to support; a company with more than one hundred employees whose jobs supported their families; and dozens more vendors, subcontractors, bankers and such who relied on us for part of their business. In many ways, surrender seemed sensible.

With the echoes of my dad's defeat ringing in my psyche, I knew well the consequences of surrender. To duck and run is foreign to me; I seem designed by nature to "go for it." Though our business troubles were not entirely of our own making, the safe options would have allowed us to escape responsibility and shift some of the burden to others, such as vendors I wouldn't have to pay in bankruptcy. That wasn't right. And if we sued, we would be stuck in the past as long as the lawsuit endured.

So, in 1976, I ignored the attorneys and the bankruptcy advocates and decided to try to lead The Neenan Company through its Casper crisis. We stayed out of court, and we set about finding new jobs, straightening out our bookkeeping, cutting costs, refocusing our strategies.

At the time my net worth was $94,000. In effect, I had lost everything I had, six times over. Yet I was trying to recoup my losses and forge ahead. Wasn't that crazy?

Maybe so, but risk is essential to a meaningful life. Not just human life, but all life. To find a new home and achieve the biological imperative of expanding its territory, an organism must leave the home it has. When a seed starts to sprout, it doesn't have a weather forecast.

Overall, I believe in prudent risk—an unflinching assessment of what's to lose versus what's to gain—but in the Casper crisis, my determination was intrinsic as much as it was intellectual. By the time we got our business and our books straightened out enough to see exactly how much we had lost, we were making money again.

That's wonderful, but it's not the most important result. The numerical outcome of an endeavor is simply a measurement, and keeping score does not add meaning to life. The fact that going for it on fourth down can achieve a positive outcome is less important to me than the fact that consistently doing so builds strength and expertise.

What I learn from the effort of endeavor is the most important outcome. That's growth—learning while you strive. From Casper, I learned a lot about sound financial management, wise job selection, leadership by example, and focused business strategy. The lessons have been incorporated into the core of my being, and I've called on them when other challenges came my way.

The necessity of risk is a cornerstone of human wisdom: Nothing ventured, nothing gained, goes the ancient axiom. Surely everyone would agree that a life spent sitting on the couch is spiritually, as well as physically, pointless.

Nonetheless, there we sit, far too many of us, mired in existential angst, if not outright surrender. We dream of writing songs, or painting landscapes, or starting companies, or seeing the world, or trying out for Jeopardy. And still we sit. What if we lose money? What if people laugh at us? Thoreau's observation that most people lead lives of "quiet desperation" seems even more true now than it was two centuries ago.

The more action we take, the more often we will face trouble. That idea seems perversely dangerous to anyone squirming anxiously within a life of quiet desperation. Isn't the whole point of life to avoid trouble?

No.

We grow up learning that embarrassment and fear are experiences we must avoid. I believe we are all magnificent, but we only discover this when we take a stand during adversity. If we only find our magnificence when we are truly challenged, then embarrassment and fear are the universe's way of telling us we're engaged.

Courage is the quality that enables risk taking. Aristotle called it the first virtue. Where do I find it? I look in the mirror. If everything I try fails, how will I feel about myself? Almost always, I am reminded of the notion that we regret the things we don't do far more than the things we do. But doubters fret that they can't predict the outcome. In reality, we never can.

There is a difference between courage and foolhardiness. Let me use skydiving as an analogy. If you jump out of an airplane without a parachute, that's stupid. If you do so without first taking a lesson, that's naïve and rash. If there's a good reason for you to jump and you're well-prepared, but you duck it, then fear is ruling your choice.

To me, courage simply means commitment plus doubt. I had no idea that the strategies I adopted, personal and corporate, would succeed as well as they did when I led The Neenan Company through the Casper disaster. I only knew that I had to do something, despite my fears that I was about to fail at a lifetime goal of success, wealth, and family financial security.

Did I doubt whether we could pull out of the hole we were in? Of course, I did. It would take incredible naivete to think otherwise, but I exercised the courage to go ahead anyway.

Commitment is simply the personal drive to see something through despite doubt. Doubt is not only inherent to taking risks, it's realistic: Nobody succeeds at every venture. If you have no doubts, either your attempt is modest, or you are being rash and need a reality check.

You have to passionately want what you seek. If I find myself knowing what I need to do, but somehow I don't do it, maybe my desire isn't as strong as it should be. Am I telling myself the truth about how much I want this? I wanted with every cell of my being to save The Neenan Company and my family from bankruptcy.

Among the many freedoms humans enjoy is the ability to frame our own feelings. That includes fear and doubt, which I shaped in a fashion some might call euphemistic when I wrote a letter to my bonding agent in 1976. I called the Casper struggle a "challenge," rather than a catastrophe. Why shouldn't I give my own interpretation to my personal situation? It belongs to me. Calling it a "disaster," as I do now, is wry retrospect.

It's useful to ask: What's the worst that could happen? In that case, the worst would have been pretty bad—bankruptcy; but if I had surrendered, that would have been the result anyway. I was afraid I might not succeed, but I was far more afraid of giving up. I didn't want to go to my grave with my song still in me.

Overall, I've faced at least nine crises in my life. "You counted?" a friend once asked, incredulous. Hell, yes, I counted. Each time, I chose to go for it; and, as Robert Frost put it, that has made all the difference.

Responsibility: Be the hero of your own life

No bird soars too high if he soars on his own wings.
—William Blake

Destiny is not found or discovered—it is invented.
—Peter Koestenbaum

"Mom, how much money does dad make in a year?"

"Well, six thousand dollars or so."

"Where is he?"

"Honey, he's at work."

"No, he's not. He's down at Booches getting drunk."

I was twelve years old, standing in our kitchen in Columbia, trying to map the universe, now that my dad had lost the fruit stand and was back driving a sales route for Nabisco. Though I didn't totally understand the adult world, it looked like my brothers and sisters and I never had new clothes, because the money went down my dad's throat in the afternoon when he ought to be at work.

"David, he might stop off after work and have a beer or two," my mom explained, gently. I shook my head. I didn't buy that.

"When I grow up, I'm going to make lots of money," I announced. "And I'm going to bring it home."

Starting then, that's just what I've done. That moment was a conscious realization of something that might seem harsh for a twelve-year-old, but I see it as a great gift: I would have to make my own way. Please understand my twelve-year-old, single-minded focus on money; at the time, I saw it as the only tool to escape our circumstances. And that's exactly what it is, a tool.

My dad was a World War II veteran, an adventurer who drove a Model T west, then made his way to Alaska and did aerial photography for Howard Hughes. He wound up a Nabisco salesman. Once, he had helped win the war against the Nazis in North Africa; now, he purveyed saltines and graham crackers in a seventy-mile radius around Columbia.

We shuttled from one rental house to another until we bought a three-story clapboard on Rollins Street and rented out the top two floors; we six boys slept in bunks in the same bedroom. In my extended family, we were the only ones who struggled to make house payments. My mom's dad was one of the most successful home builders in Kansas City. All of my dad's siblings became millionaires, but not him. Our circumstances would have been meager, even if he hadn't hit the bar on the way home.

As an adult, I long ago made peace with my father and his legacy to me. As a boy, I had determined at a very early age to make my own way, on my own terms, for me and mine. When I made that heartfelt announcement to my mother, the important point was not that I would make buckets of money, but that I would use it for my family.

At first, I just wanted enough money to buy clothes. I started my business career by selling newspaper subscriptions. Back then a jocular term for boys like me was "paper smeller," which gives you an idea of how little regard there was for such work then. (And now.)

My first success was represented by a pair of shoes. I bought the shoes using my own money, a fifty-dollar prize I won by selling one hundred, one-dollar monthly subscriptions to the local paper, the *Missourian*—more than any other paper seller.

A simple pair of shoes doesn't seem like much, but in 1956 I was a very proud eighth-grader, walking down the alley behind my house with a brand new pair of Buster Browns from Gene Glenn's Shoes downtown. There was nothing very fancy about them—they were just sturdy, dark brown, everyday footwear; but wearing them was an emotional experience I still remember. I've many, many more shoes now, but I haven't forgotten that first pair I bought myself. If you have never experienced scarcity, you'll never understand or appreciate abundance.

It was my first taste of the feeling you get when you pursue something passionately and succeed. Food, clothing, and shelter are the basic necessities of human life, and creating the wherewithal to put good shoes on my feet was a heady taste of existential fulfillment for a young boy. The experience crystallized a profound realization that transformed my life: I could take responsibility for myself and my desires.

After that, I spent most of my summers working. I'd mow lawns (my first paid job at fifty cents a lawn), paint houses, and sell newspapers. From eighth grade on, my parents never bought me clothes. Even though I was not a very good student, and I wasn't on my best behavior most of the time, my mother told me, "David, I have faith in you. You'll do fine."

In the dictionary, responsibility has many definitions. The one I find most meaningful is this: Able to answer for one's conduct and obligations.

That's the principle I learned at age twelve. If I had a desire for shoes other than those my parents supplied, I had an obligation to fulfill that desire myself. I had become the hero of my own life, a phrase I use to depict taking responsibility as an opportunity rather than a chore.

Life brings us the chance every day to make this choice. Most days, the choices are incremental rather than dramatic. If my blood pressure is up a bit, do I go for a bike ride rather than lunch at a pizza joint? If the budget is tight, do I pass up my mid-morning, triple-tall mocha? Sometimes the challenges to responsibility are dramatic, as they were for me during the Casper crisis in 1976.

I believe that we have an obligation to the universe to be responsible; we were not put here to lie about and, as the Chinese put it, wait for a roast duck to fly in our mouths. But there's also a huge personal benefit: Claiming responsibility gives us power over our lives. Putting shoes on my feet is just a simple example.

If you are a father, responsibility means taking care of your health (not smoking a pack of cigarettes a day, as I was in 1976) and being there for your kids' gymnastics meets. If you are a husband, it means supporting your wife's independent activities. If you are a citizen, it means being an informed voter. If you are a business owner, it means making the decisions necessary to preserve and grow the business—and acquiring the best possible information to do so.

The line between victim and hero is distinct. Even though people often equivocate, I don't think there's much confusion about it. We have no trouble discerning where others should take responsibility for themselves. It should be the same for ourselves.

In my early twenties, I made a more concrete choice to take responsibility when I entered Officers Candidate School in the Army. Remember how I muddled my way through high school and my first stab at college? I didn't flunk out; I didn't distinguish myself. During the first class at OCS, it became clear that my previous approach wouldn't be good enough.

The instructor, Captain John H. Crittenden, introduced himself and then said, "Gentlemen, look to your right. Now, look to your left. Six months from now, only a few of you will still be sitting here. It's your choice." There's that term again—choice. I promised myself then that I would still be there in six months—and I was. It was the first time I'd played by the rules and succeeded.

Taking responsibility is a kind of personal fitness best maintained by frequent exercise. The difference lies in our response to events. Instead of asking what somebody did to me, I can ask: How do I choose to answer this challenge? Instead of asking what someone else should do about my problem, I can ask: What can I do to improve the situation? The answers to these questions mark the distinction between victim and hero.

It's interesting how some remarks stay with you forever. One day in junior high school, my first girlfriend asked me, "David, why do you wear the same three shirts all the time?"

It was because I was buying my own wardrobe with my own money, of course, and at that moment I had just three shirts. I can still see myself as that very young man, and I can still feel the burn of disgrace I experienced. I made a point of earning money to buy a few more shirts. In fact, now my wife asks, "David, how come you have so many shirts?"

So many people see responsibilities as burdens. To me they represent the gift of freedom, and all my shirts still symbolize taking responsibility for myself. As Sartre put it, "Freedom is what you do with what's been done to you."

Chapter 4

The Stone Wall: Four things you can do

Man is condemned to be free; because once thrown into the world, he is responsible for everything he does. —Jean-Paul Sartre

The opportunity to be responsible is easily met on sunlit garden lanes with robins singing in our ears, but we gain little then. Moments of hardship and difficulty are the times when we strengthen the muscle of responsibility. Only through challenge do we grow.

I had the chance to experience this vividly in my late twenties, and the episode set me on my path as a business owner. On the surface, my life looked splendid, the prototypical first full chapter in the American dream. It was 1973. I'd returned from Australia and married the girl I left behind, Sharon. I had a good job working for my uncle Bill's construction company in Kansas City. Sharon was bringing home a steady salary as a teacher, and we lived on that and saved the rest. Isn't that what we're all supposed to set sail toward—a good job, young marriage, wise savings, a steady upward path?

Sure, I was experiencing frustrations. As a relative of the company owner I was viewed with distrust by other workers: Was

I capable or just enjoying nepotism? On the other hand, I wasn't a member of Bill's immediate family. I wanted to own something, but when I asked to buy stock in his company, my uncle told me there was one problem: "You've got the wrong last name, David." His sons could. I couldn't.

When Sharon became pregnant I began to worry about my future, our future, our not-yet-born kids' future. I invited an insurance salesman to stop by, and, in the course of the evening, I started to ask him a question about the differences between insurance options. "If I buy term life, can I convert to—" I couldn't get the last word out. Gobbledygook emerged from my mouth. I tried the question again. Same result.

Something was wrong with me. My older sister Barbara, by then a psychiatrist, made an appointment for me with Dr. Mark Dodge, a highly respected physician at St. Luke's in Kansas City. He examined and probed me, sent me for a CT-scan, took blood, gave me balance tests; I was tested up and down for a couple of hours. Then he said to come back in three days, and we'd discuss the results.

Three days later I sat down with Dr. Dodge. "David, I have good news and bad news. The good news is, there's nothing physically wrong with you. No tumor, no brain dysfunction."

I tried to digest this as positive.

"So what's wrong with me? What's the bad news?"

"You have hit…" he paused a moment, "…the stone wall of life." That's when he smacked the palm of his left hand with his right fist. It was dramatic. I was puzzled, to say the least. But I asked a question that typifies my approach to life.

"Well, what do I do?"

"You have three choices," Dr. Dodge told me. "First, you can be like Timothy Leary—tune in, turn on, and drop out. Lots of people are doing that these days." (This was 1973.)

I shook my head. "What's my second option?"

"Well, you can find a comfortable spot in the wall, accept your fate, and perhaps become a functioning alcoholic."

I didn't want to do that. My dad had. His misery was profound.

"And the third?"

"Well, if you're lucky or determined enough, you can keep hitting the wall, and hitting the wall, until you bounce over it."

"Then what?"

"Then, some day, another stone wall," he told me. "And if you're really lucky, you'll hit five or six stone walls in your life."

Lucky? What great news: Hit a wall, whack yourself a few times, bounce over it, head off for another wall. Yikes. No wonder sea squirts send out holdfasts and stay put.

Though I didn't wind up in a psych ward popping Valium (many people do, and our medical system these days makes it all too easy), I'd had a breakdown. I've since come to recognize such events as priceless turning points.

Dr. Dodge was one of those key people you meet on the road of life—someone with special insight at a critical time. What the universe expects of us is to listen, then act; and for me the message was clear. If I was going to get over this wall, I'd have to leave Kansas City. Geographic change can be an escape from responsibility, but it can also represent genuine steps forward on life's path. A month later, Sharon miscarried, and I thought, if ever the universe was sending a message, this is it. We need to find a business to own; we need a new start; and we'll do both of those things best somewhere else.

Though Dr. Dodge offered me three options, I've since come to recognize there are four. Moments of challenge almost never have just one possible response, so here we are meeting our old friend, choice; and now we see a clearer picture of what challenges entail. When you find yourself at a point of conflict in life, it's almost always with another person or human institution. The more painful the situation—an execrable job, an abusive spouse, intolerable political systems—the more harsh these four options seem.

- Change yourself: In my case, I could have reordered my desires and ambitions and accepted long-term employment as a valuable midlevel manager at my uncle's company—but not as president or partner. In the case of, say, an alcoholic, you could enter treatment and begin recovery.

- Change the system: If your job is unsatisfactory, you could transfer to a different area, ask for different responsibilities, buy the company, or start your own. If you've grown weary of a three-year courtship, you could get married. If your diet and exercise plan isn't lowering your blood pressure, you could switch to yoga and a different nutrition plan. If your country is enslaved you could change its political system—Thomas Jefferson, Mahatma Gandhi, and Nelson Mandela did.

- Get out: You want to get married, but your three-year fiancée doesn't? Leave. Abusive spouse won't get treatment? Same.

- Suffer: Stick around and be beaten occasionally. Set aside your lifelong dreams and keep punching that time clock. Drink yourself into oblivion. Accept tyranny. At least the trains run on time.

When Sharon and I packed up for Colorado and bought a construction company, we were, in effect, choosing all of the first three options—we changed ourselves, changed the system, and we got out. I know these are the sorts of actions many people consider out of their reach. Too risky. Who has the money? "I can't do that," goes the standard excuse. I've come to believe that the word *can't* almost always means *won't*.

And *can't* is the magic password to door number four, the suffering option. Millions of people make this choice every day. Battered wives pick themselves up and stay home, embittered employees dream of success they will never find, alcoholics and their families endure misery and ruin.

Pointing out these choices is quintessentially existential, and it strikes many people as unbearably harsh. Because the first three options seem so difficult to most people (and they often are difficult!), the common sentiment is that this way of looking at things dooms most people to suffering. If they *can't* (there's that word) avail themselves of any of the first three choices, what else is there? Damn those existentialists! Let's go have a beer. Let's pray.

I would say to them that we all enjoy the option of changing ourselves at any time. Yes, I know a person five feet tall can't magically add two more feet and become a basketball star, but there are plenty of short basketball stars. People with depression can get treatment. Alcoholics can stop drinking. Batterers can undergo anger management therapy.

Changing the system or getting out are two options more available than most people think, too. Millions of people fled the Soviet Union; Lech Walesa led Poland to freedom. Most Americans have ancestors who did one or the other or both.

To me it's wonderful that there are three positive options—three ways to initiate change—and only one negative choice. A three-to-one chance of making things better! The universe is offering fabulous odds here.

That makes hitting the wall a splendid event, and that's what Dr. Dodge was telling me. Such a breakdown is the visible outcome of *perturbation*, the word used to describe trouble that increasingly disrupts an individual or organization. It often takes the shape of outright crisis, such as the one I had five years later in Casper. These are the memorable moments in life when we may—that's the key word, *may*—have a breakthrough. Three of the four options represent some form of breakthrough, and this is what nature wants.

Breakthroughs don't come in increments, and they require persistence. Remember when you set out to learn to ride a bike? We struggle and fall, struggle and fall—and then we manage to stay upright and get all the way down the driveway. Suddenly, we get it. Breakthrough. Falling down was painful. But it was a necessary step before the cognitive (and kinetic) leap into the new skill of bike riding.

This process is universal. Most people make some stab at one of the three change options several times before they succeed: alcoholics get counseling two or three times, battered wives make several attempts to leave, revolutions start and fail. Nature itself operates this way. Caterpillars start shaking and agitating within their cocoons before they break free as butterflies. IBM was shaken to the core by Apple's personal computers until it started making its own; then it dominated the industry for twenty years, until Dell and other competitors bounced IBM into another new shape as a server, systems, and information services company. Boeing lost federal funding for the SST, and was forced to gamble everything on a radical new plane, the 747, which became the most widely recognized industrial product on the planet.

I describe perturbations, such as my experience hitting the wall in Kansas City, as upsets that offer the opportunity to see the truth. When you're perturbed and aware, it means that an opportunity for a breakthrough may be at hand. You can take a profound step into a different order of personal existence. Or you can choose option number four and continue to suffer.

Having a breakthrough doesn't mean you've had your last breakdown. Far from it—and you should hope not. I've had any number of breakdowns and breakthroughs in my life; most of the stories in this book are about them. I can't say they ever become pleasant experiences. The cliché says: no pain, no gain. I would add to this that pain is a passionate, deeply felt experience; if you feel pain, you're engaged in life. The first breakdown is a chance to gain confidence that you can reach a breakthrough. The realization is liberating.

I am sometimes asked, "What if I've never hit the wall?" I perceive people who lead untrammeled lives to be woefully unlucky or blissfully unconscious. I'd say, find a way to expose yourself to risk. In order to claim you're the hero of your own life, you have to say yes to challenge. As Mark Twain put it, "Necessity is the mother of taking chances." If perturbation doesn't find you, go find it. If you haven't hit a wall, go look for one. Try to remember that bad news can actually be good news. Then get on that scary, exhilarating tide and paddle as hard as you can.

Chapter 5

Growth: You can't learn less

In times of change learners inherit the earth, while the learned find themselves beautifully equipped to deal with a world that no longer exists. —Eric Hoffer

The only man who makes no mistakes is the man who never does anything. —Teddy Roosevelt

Most of the best things that ever came my way seemed, at first, as if they might be the worst. Each event challenged me to open my eyes, assess my mistakes, understand how I had made them, and change myself.

And that's the essence of learning: undergoing an experience from which you develop the capacity to achieve something you could not before.

Simply acquiring information is not learning. Reading a book (including this one), taking a class, talking to a wise elder—these are worthy activities, indeed; but they constitute exposure to information. The difference here is between knowing and doing. Knowing is technical: You can "know" *http*, and lots of people do.

But that doesn't mean you can create a successful website, any more than knowing how to type means you can write a book.

Taking action is the pathway to learning. It's the only path.

The 1976 Casper crisis was an example of this. The Neenan Company had bid on a construction job in Casper, Wyoming, which is three hundred miles from our home base in Fort Collins. It seemed like a simple job—build a fifty-thousand-square-foot racquet and sports club—and we won the bid. Casper was in the midst of an oil and gas boom; The Neenan Company had grown from the almost-dormant Butler Building dealer I'd bought in 1973 to a bustling young construction firm. We thought Casper's growth was a great fit for ours.

The job turned into a disaster. It's not a coincidence that Wyoming is one of the most challenging environments—climatically, economically and socially—in North America. Things went haywire by fits and starts. For instance, we priced the job too quickly, working with an architect new to us, who changed more than a dozen specifications between the initial drawings and the construction blueprints. We were unaware of geologic challenges in the area, were unprepared for poor weather, estimated work time and costs poorly, and wound up having to pour some concrete twice.

About the same time I experienced a painful personal catastrophe. I was playing racquetball, a sport in which I competed ferociously, and in the middle of one game an errant shot hit me right in the groin. Ironically, it was my own shot—I'd rebounded the ball off the back wall. After gasping in pain on the floor for a few minutes, I got up and finished the game.

After the game I went to the hospital. They gave me some Demerol and told me to apply ice; my doc, Peter Standard, strongly suggested I go home and stay still for a week. I did, sort of, for two days. Remember that picture taken then? It tells the whole story: I'm propped in bed with ice in my lap, phone at my ear, cigarette in my mouth, *Wall Street Journal* in hand. The high-flying young entrepreneur was not going to let a little sports mishap interfere with his 24/7 dedication to business.

That year The Neenan Company's sales goal was $2.5 million, and we were about $800,000 short. At that very moment, the contract for the Casper job needed my signature. It was worth $839,000. So, after those two days of quasi-rest, I hopped in a car with our top salesman and drove six hours to Casper, barely a week after the accident. By the time I got back, I was in excruciating pain again, so I returned to the emergency room. My testicle was abscessed—it had to go. By refusing to sit still, I had let the swelling cut off the blood supply to the injury. When I got out of surgery, Dr. Standard told me I must have cut off the blood supply to my brain, too.

We made our annual sales goal, but the bottom line for business isn't revenue, it's profit. (That's why the U.S. government had to bail out General Motors—they had demonstrated the old business adage that while volume thrills, margin kills. They sold millions of poor-quality cars and lost money doing it.) It was clear our losses in Casper were severe, and we had another project at the same time that was in trouble. Rather than sue or file for bankruptcy, I went to my banker—Tom Gleason, with whom I'd struck up a relationship when I arrived in town—and Butler Manufacturing, the company whose structural steel we used. Butler put up the money, in a five-year note, to finish the Casper job.

At the same time, I sat down to take personal inventory. I'd begun to reflect on my life when I left the hospital minus one testicle. If ever there is a time for a man to take stock of things, it's when he halves the biological organ that makes him male. The Neenan Company and its president had both been guilty of over-reaching, so I refocused on the basics that had gotten us to our modest level of pre-Casper success:

- Find work.

- Do work.

- Measure the results (keep score).

With the guidance of Don Bell, a workout officer at our bank, we also instituted some specific changes inspired by the mistakes we made in Casper. No more distant jobs in unfamiliar places. No more bidding on the basis of preliminary drawings. We prepared regular fiscal assessments that included weekly cashflow statements, timely income statements and balance sheets, and monthly backlog compilations. All helped to provide accurate, timely measurements of where we were. And we adopted a new financial goal—profit rather than revenue.

I also made a point of cataloguing, on paper, the mistakes I'd made. I still have that letter I sent to our bonding agent back then, listing our mistakes, what I'd learned, and the changes we'd made as a result. "This has been the most rigorous challenge of my career," I wrote.

The whole episode began the process of transforming The Neenan Company from an average builder of prefab industrial buildings into a lean, innovative, design-build company that approaches construction as a group of artisans working together to satisfy our clients' needs. It was a priceless set of lessons.

There were some personal lessons that year, too. I had to heal my racquetball injury, and I couldn't do it overnight. At first, I had to take hot baths every two hours; then every four hours; then five times a day; and so on, for forty-five days. I had to irrigate the surgical wound with hydrogen peroxide—not fun. The hot baths helped relieve the discomfort, and I developed an affinity for pulp fiction, devouring the adventures of John D. McDonald's hero Travis McGee.

I began to take better care of myself and my spirit; whatever aura the leader of a company radiates is what the company itself will adopt. I inaugurated my exploration of innovative business and personal growth. And I recognized that mistakes have a purpose.

Shortly after Casper I began to discover the teachings of Buckminster Fuller. Bucky was an engineer, a philosopher, a humanitarian, a visionary—and a genuine human being. He is famous for creating the geodesic dome, and conceived the idea of "Spaceship Earth" in 1927, long before there was any such thing as a spaceship, or a concept of earth as a whole.

Bucky called mistakes "great moments." If that's so, then my Casper adventure was a world-class set of great moments. One way to look at it is that I came within a whisker of catastrophic business and personal failure. Great, huh?

The other perspective is that I paid $670,000 to learn how to run a lean, intelligent, forward-thinking, and accountable business. In the years since, The Neenan Company has built more than $1 billion worth of buildings, so the tuition was less than one-tenth of 1 percent—pretty modest.

I was lucky enough to meet Bucky shortly before he died in 1983. He urged his listeners to maintain a lifelong openness to new ideas.

"If you have the courage to try something new, you don't learn less," Bucky said. "You can only and always learn more."

I've condensed his statement to: "You don't learn less." If I stay reasonably alert to the world around me, every day brings something new. It's a great way to live. If you are always learning, and open to it, you're certainly never bored. And, as Eric Hoffer pointed out, you're better equipped for the constantly changing world we live in.

Though making mistakes is not the only way to learn, it is clearly the most memorable and lasting. Luckily, we all make mistakes all the time. I know I do. Though it'd be nice not to, it's folly to think that's possible. My goal is to correct, not protect. Asked who his hero was, Bucky replied that it's whoever points out to him that he's blind to something—someone who makes visible the invisible.

The usefulness of mistakes doesn't mean one should court catastrophe. Many enterprises demand that disastrous errors be avoided: Do you want your 747 pilot to make a "mistake" on takeoff? Imagine what would have happened to the space program if NASA had launched a rocket right into Miami. It wouldn't be all right for The Neenan Company to make a "mistake" on the beam strength necessary to support a ceiling. That's why there are such things as flight simulators, engineering standards, product testing and computer-simulation programs.

A learning, productive life requires a capacity to take personal risks and overcome fear of failure, rejection, and embarrassment. If your dream is to become a singer, yet you avoid getting up on stage because you fear the embarrassment of a wrong note, your dream will remain just a whim.

Recognizing and correcting specific mistakes—gaining experience—isn't all that's needed, either. W. Edwards Deming was the brilliant theorist who led Japan to industrial prominence after World War II, and his influence rings through to today's global auto hierarchy. As Deming put it, "Experience plus theory equals profound results. If experience is such a great teacher, why isn't General Motors the best auto manufacturer?" General Motors focused on factors other than quality and manufacturing efficiency, and Toyota, whose theory was continuous quality improvement, became the world's top carmaker.

Just because you get a "successful" score doesn't mean you have learned. A while back, I was invited to teach a leadership class at Colorado State University. The class members were freshmen who had shown great potential. At the end of the first session, several of the students came up to me to ask, "Please tell me what I have to do to get an A in this class." Getting an A is a technical issue. Leadership is not. I felt like telling them to go find another class.

In Casper, The Neenan Company got a huge amount of experience. When we adopted a new theory—focus on profitability rather than gross revenue—we started making money.

We can learn from success. Our rebound from Casper solidified the merits of our new strategies. Strap on a pair of skis and the exhilaration of successful turns creates a body memory of what went into them. Rather than let your six-year-old fall off her new bike twenty-five times, you hold the seat for her, or install training wheels. Continuous negative reinforcement is good for nobody, and the capitalist marketplace has mechanisms to prevent this, such as the bankruptcy I narrowly avoided.

Today I sum up the whole Casper episode by saying I had the glorious opportunity to go broke—horribly broke—in my mid-thirties. But that was just the beginning.

Purpose: Clarity is the key

The real act of discovery consists not in finding new lands but in seeing with new eyes. —Marcel Proust

All progress begins by telling the truth. —Lee Brower

Most of my lessons have resulted from my own experience. But on a drilling rig in the Australian outback, someone else's trouble prompted a life-changing realization for me.

I was out in the Simpson Desert on a rig owned by Zapata Oil Drilling and Exploration. We were miles from the nearest settlement, dozens of miles from a town, hundreds of miles from any city. The desert was largely featureless; during the day the sun blazed down, and at night the sky was an infinite blanket of stars. I'd come to Australia seeking my fortune, in the old-fashioned sense of the word: not just money but a path in life.

The nearest town, Birdsville, is accurately described by an Australian travel guide as a famous outback township which is little more than a pub and few houses. "It is hard to imagine any place in Australia which evokes quite the sense of loneliness and isolation as this tiny settlement at the northern end of the notorious and dangerous Birdsville track," says the *Sydney Herald*. "Located over 1600 kilometers west of Brisbane in the vast Diamantina Shire, Birdsville sits on the edge of the Simpson Desert and operates like some kind of mysterious magnet to people who want to go to the most isolated place on the continent."

I had been drawn by that magnet, and in the weird perspective young men use to view the world, working on an oil rig at the end of nowhere was glamorous. I was handling the "tongs," and a luckless compatriot was on the drillworks floor with me, handling chains. One night about 2:00 AM, he got a hand caught in the chain and lopped off four of his fingers. He made a simple, half-second mistake, and the result was sudden and brutal. I had been a medic in the Army and helped treat him, not that there was much to be done other than to stop the bleeding, protect the wound, and treat for shock. I applied a tourniquet, and we took him to a doctor in Birdsville, but there was little the doc could do for him, either—his drilling career was over. Back we went to the rig, and I inherited his job. "OK, Neenan," the driller told me the next night, "you're on chains."

It was a promotion, believe it or not—more responsibility, better pay. So, there I was on a drilling rig in the Australian outback, and I started thinking.

I was twenty-five. After completing Officer Candidate School and mustering out of the Army, I graduated cum laude from the University of Missouri with a degree in marketing and business administration, and I began to feel restless. I didn't know what I wanted to do, didn't know what I wanted to be. I had a great job offer from McGraw-Hill in New York, but I was intrigued by the idea of emigrating to Australia. I'd read up on it in the library—it seemed like the last frontier, a place where people were authentic and kept their word. So I sewed $700 in my Army fatigue jacket and spent a last night with my girlfriend, Sharon, who dropped me off the next morning on Interstate 70 and kissed me goodbye. I headed to California to find a way to the South Seas.

Over the next few months, I made my way from California to Hawaii, where I got a job as a brick carrier so I could buy passage on a ship. In Fiji, the next stop, I watched over a coconut plantation for a month. It sounds exotic, but really there wasn't much to do on Fiji except watch them load copra on boats. Oh, and drink kava, the local liquor—it makes your lips numb, if that tells you anything. The Fijians loved to go wild boar hunting, and we did that, too, a strenuous and dangerous pastime. Otherwise it was a pretty dull month.

Eventually, I made my way to Australia, my promised land, where I worked at odd jobs here and there, hitchhiked across country, had colorful adventures, and wound up in the outback on a drilling rig, in the middle of the night, replacing a guy who'd lost four fingers on the exact same job the night before. At least I was exercising responsibility for my life.

Or was I?

I was halfway around the world, in the middle of nowhere, a rig roustabout, getting paid $1.37 an hour. I was watching fingers fly off in the night. It was more than two hours to the nearest hotel. Beer-guzzling and bar-fighting were the local sports. I thought I'd come to the last frontier, but instead I just found a very remote place with lots of heat, dust, and wide open space.

What was I doing in Australia? I was avoiding the truth about myself and what I wanted.

I had performed a maneuver that recovering alcoholics call a "geographic change." Daily life is a drag, things don't feel right—

that shapeless, insistent anxiety that means you are ignoring the call of your life—think I'll pack the car and head to Vegas. Anything to avoid the changes that really need to be made.

Oh, I had some fun on my journey Down Under. I tell colorful tales about it. I learned a few lessons that have stood me in good stead ever since. But one cannot be a passionate, purposeful vagabond; at least, I cannot.

I was separated as far as I could be—physically, emotionally, financially, and spiritually—from where I had come, trying to "find myself." And that night on the drilling platform, I realized I was still the same guy. I hadn't changed; only my surroundings had. I'd been looking for freedom *from*, but what I needed was freedom *to*, and the only individual who could create that was me.

What I wanted was back here in the States—and so was the person I wanted to share that life with, Sharon. I wanted to have a family; I wanted to accumulate wealth so I could provide for my family, extended family, and friends; and I wanted a spouse who would love and support and challenge me.

I was not put on this earth by chance, but for a purpose, and what I was doing in Australia did not serve my purpose. My first night on chains was my last night on the drilling rig; the next day I quit and headed back to the States. The value of that moment of clarity has been immeasurable: The purpose I set myself has guided my life ever since. That purpose is not the only one of my life, nor should acquiring wealth, even if it is for the good of your family, be the only purpose of anyone's life. What matters is having purpose and passion, and it matters a lot.

There may be plenty of people for whom a job in the outback fits their purpose. But that night on the drilling rig I told myself the truth—my truth. My new understanding was just an evolutionary leap on a lifelong path of learning. This word *truth* is fraught with perilous weight in human thought. Bucky Fuller calls truth "progressively diminishing error," which means that each version of it more closely approaches real accuracy, but probably never reaches it. In physics, to pick a scientific example, we thought we'd exposed the deepest mysteries of matter with the discovery of atomic particles—and then quarks turned up. Microbiologists thought mapping the human genome would unveil the workings of human biology; then they found that it's an infinitely more complicated web of genes, amino acids and their interactions.

Umberto Maturana says that "The Truth," a declaration of terms and conditions some people try to force on others, is almost always just a demand for obedience. This phenomenon is a common occurrence in religious doctrine. Many zealots in several faiths declare it as truth that women are inferior to men. Is that the truth for you?

No one else can declare the truth for you. It must be based on your own real experiences, heartfelt passions, and honest assessments. And it's important to keep in mind that all "truth," mine and others', is filtered by what are called paradigms.

Several years ago, standing before an audience of two hundred people in New York, magician David Copperfield told them he was about to make the Statue of Liberty disappear. It was clearly visible through the arches on the outdoor stage; Copperfield closed the curtains between the arches, proceeded with a series of flourishes and preparations, then reopened the curtains. Presto! No statue. Utterly gone. Hundreds of people could not believe their own eyes.

How did he do that? It was incredibly simple: While the curtains were closed, he triggered a gear that slowly and imperceptibly moved the entire theater and stage, shifting the angle just enough that the statue was hidden behind the arch on one side. He changed the framework in which his audience was viewing the world, but they did not know it. He had subjected them to a paradigm shift.

Most of the frameworks in which we see and interpret what's around us are not made and altered so deliberately. Instead, cultural, educational or even biological forces are behind them. Cats have difficulty seeing stationary prey because their long evolution as hunters has conditioned them to look for dinner moving sideways, and their visual systems evolved in accordance with that. Thus, even though a meal may be sitting in plain view in front of them, they don't see it because they can't see it. We see what we see, we don't see what we don't see. It's possible and common to be blind and innocent in the face of the obvious.

The old saying goes, I'll believe it when I see it. The paradigmatic version is, I'll see it when I believe it. That makes these frameworks incredibly powerful determinants of what we see in our world. Have you ever declared that you couldn't possibly get up on stage in front of a thousand people and give an impromptu speech? There's no way you can learn to ski? Leave your job? Get along with your mother?

When you become aware of a paradigm, it often represents a chance to do something new. I had such a shift in the outback. Old paradigm: I was a restless young man who needed new geographic frontiers to achieve fulfillment. New paradigm: The frontiers I needed to explore were back at home.

My friend Marshall Thurber based his path to wealth on a new perspective. Rather than looking at San Francisco's stock of rundown Victorian houses as eyesores in need of "urban renewal," he began restoring them in the early 1970s. Repainted in their original vivid hues, these "painted ladies" sold magnificently.

We all have paradigms; they are necessary for us to make sense of the infinitely complex universe we inhabit. The best we can do is to seek experiences that expose us to other ways of viewing the world, and keep an open mind.

A key to this is honest feedback from others. No one can tell you your truth, but outside perspectives are crucial. Imagine if I'd had a wise elder sit down with me in the Australian desert and point out that my current path had nothing to do with the call of my heart. "David, your skills are entrepreneurial and motivational. And I hear you saying you want to build family, community, and wealth to take care of them. This doesn't look like the way to do that." No such advice came my way, but the universe sent me an experience that served the same purpose. Luckily, it wasn't me who suffered the industrial accident!

The realization that came to me in the Australian outback was a moment of clarity; I knew what I wanted to accomplish, and who I wanted to do it with. That clarity has lent energy and strength to my efforts ever since. That night it became clear I needed to have my own business.

Clarity is just what it sounds like—simple, comprehensible understanding. It is one of the fundamental prerequisites to any achievement. Clear instructions produce clear results. Clear data lead to clear decisions. The more clearly you define your goal, the more likely you will accomplish it, whether you are communicating with others or setting your own objectives.

Clarity is not the same thing as singlemindedness. That's zealotry—the foundation of fundamentalism. Clarity is expressing an objective simply and understandably.

At The Neenan Company, we have sometimes lost work because of internal confusion about whether we really wanted the job; we acted as disaffected wayfarers rather than committed business people. The lack of clarity telegraphs a confusing message to our potential clients, significantly reducing the power of our presentation. So we try to align our passions beforehand and make sure we really want a contract before we go after it.

While I have framed my discussion of clarity in terms of aspiration, the concept applies to an infinite number of human experiences that range from everyday to extraordinary. If you need directions to get to San Francisco, will "Head west" suffice? Want to bake a cake: "Mix flour, chocolate and eggs." Feelings: "Sure, Suzy, I like you well enough." We each use thousands of windows to frame our world, and each window needs to be as free of grime and distortion as possible.

I believe the broader my experience of the world around us—the broader my paradigms—the more powerful my realizations will be. Travel is a matchless way to expand your horizons; and, even though I realize that what I want is back here at home, I have continued to travel the earth, both as a tourist and while presenting my "Business & You" workshops. I've been to more than fifty countries and have visited all six inhabited continents. But, to borrow a thought from Eric Hoffer, no amount of knowledge and experience substitutes for the ability to read the landscape of your own heart.

Chapter 7

Preparation: Action must be based on good foundations

Research is a blind date with knowledge. —Will Henry

Every problem is an opportunity, yes, but encountering a problem doesn't necessarily mean you can solve it or make a worthwhile enterprise of it. After recognition comes information-gathering: Identify the potential enterprise and investigate whether a need exists that you can, in fact, meet. In my case, after my return from Australia in 1970, it was clear that I needed to go into business for myself. But what business and where?

Answers to such questions come from what's called market research. It's the key to making sure you put your money and energy to use in an arena where it's likely to bear fruit. In legal terms, it's due diligence: Talk to people who know the field, find out what potential customers think, visit with suppliers. Good stock analysts do the same, sometimes uncovering a company's business trouble before its own executives know. This sort of laying the groundwork for later action is key to much of successful endeavor, but it is rarely visible in our culture so focused on instant gratification. We've forgotten Edison's axiom that genius is 99 percent perspiration, 1 percent inspiration.

When the true aspirations of my life dawned on me in the Australian outback, I realized I had made a mistake common in business: A flawed assessment of the initial condition that preceded action. I thought the longings that dogged me demanded a picaresque journey to the other side of the earth. I "misread the data," to use a common explanation.

According to W. Edwards Deming, 85 percent of the results of any enterprise depend on the first 15 percent of the work. If you need to get to Tokyo, and you think you're starting the journey in Los Angeles when you're really in London—you're way off track. You might draw up the world's best blueprints and use the finest materials to build a first-class house, but if you didn't do an adequate soils analysis first and it sinks in the mud, all that excellent construction was wasted.

This is also true in cultural terms. How many people have you heard say, I can't find a decent life partner, and I've dated dozens. Where are they looking? Cocktail parties, bars, and online chat rooms.

Achieving a thorough initial assessment is called market research. Visit the territory you think you want to enter. Talk to people already successful in similar endeavors. Try your hand at entry-level efforts. Draw up alternatives and tell yourself the truth about the criteria you'll use to choose among them.

When my wife Sharon and I came to Colorado in 1973 to buy the business that became The Neenan Company, we packed up and moved in the space of two weeks. That may seem hasty. It wasn't. I didn't just step off a cliff into a new life. I had spent more than a year in research, laying the groundwork. When I finally made my decision, I had already considered and rejected many other choices.

I was working at the time for my Uncle Bill Clarkson's construction company—both sides of my family had been involved in building of various sorts for three generations—so I had an excellent perspective on that industry. In fact, when I was a boy, my grandfather Joe Gier told me, "David, I know you're going to build something some day. Just don't build houses."

Okay, no houses. I made a list of thirty businesses I might be interested in and started to sort through the list. It didn't take long to pare the list down to six (eliminating the more undesirable choices like owning a convenience store, a catfish farm or a walnut orchard), and I started to investigate those more thoroughly, measuring both the potential of the business and my own interest in it. Then, I narrowed it to three: a Butler Building franchise, a United Campground franchise, and an ammonia distributing plant.

I committed to spend thirty days looking at each of them. In some cases I shadowed a business owner for a few days. In one case, I invested $5,000 in a campground franchise that never actually opened. It turned out that it would take another $100,000 to get the campground running. I recalled John Wayne's advice to a young wrangler on a runaway horse in the movie *The Cowboys:* "There's a time to hang on, and a time to let go." Five thousand was a lot of money to lose at the time, but it was a good lesson; and I'm grateful now that I didn't wind up running RV campgrounds.

I decided to focus on a Butler Building franchise and picked three possibilities, visiting the communities in which they operated. Ultimately, I settled on a Colorado commercial construction company that was also a franchise dealer for Butler Manufacturing Co. The company was in stasis at the time and had no active clients or employees; but it did have a good name in a growing community and offered the best line of pre-engineered buildings in three counties. Under those conditions, I could start with an established business in a field with which I was familiar. None of those factors guaranteed success, but I had laid the groundwork as thoroughly as I could. And, just as it is with a physical building, the foundation is key to the long-term stability of the enterprise.

Years later, when I was a member of the Fort Collins School Board, I noticed that the district was encountering problems with older buildings that had asbestos. In the first half of the twentieth century, it was used extensively for fire, heat, and sound insulation. It's excellent for those purposes, but it is an extremely virulent carcinogen and does not belong in public buildings. We had a very difficult time finding contractors who could perform the removal work safely and effectively.

After I left the school board, I assigned someone in my company to check out the problem. It was widespread—perhaps half the buildings constructed before 1973 had asbestos in them. So we went beyond identifying the problem to investigating its potential as a business. What did customers want from removal contractors? They wanted high quality and reliability—characteristics of our existing construction business. We formed a company to enter the asbestos removal industry, starting with $60,000, and, for most of the 1980s, it was one of our fastest-growing enterprises. We called it Risk Removal. After a few years, we sold it—with a total return on investment of several million dollars. It's still in operation today under new ownership.

Market research helps in all of life's endeavors. In my early sixties, I thought I was adequately fit (the days of high stress, cigarettes, and careless lifestyle were far behind me), but an invitation to join one of the toughest bicycle races in the world presented a challenge I wasn't up to—yet. The Triple Bypass is one hundred miles of steep mountain riding, crossing three passes, with a total elevation gain of more than ten thousand feet. I resolved to do it. But I didn't just hop on my bike and head up to 11,200-foot Loveland Pass the next day, because I had a new perspective on fitness. I began with market research.

I talked to my personal trainer, who helped me create a training program. I gathered advice from friends who had done the race. I visited a bike shop and bought a high-octane composite bike specially made for over-the-road races. I read about nutrition for endurance races and changed my diet.

All that is market research. I used what I learned to prepare with a passion I'd not felt in years, and, by the morning of the Triple Bypass, I had a nearly complete sense of confidence that I could finish the race. I got on my bike at 5:00 AM and rode strong all day; the race itself was a piece of cake.

It's common for human beings to look at others' achievements and say, that's just luck. "You were just lucky that you started Risk Removal right when asbestos consciousness reached a peak." Not at all. So many have said that luck is what happens when preparation meets opportunity. I say, luck is what happens when preparation meets action. No, knowledge is not action, but it shapes action so it's more effective. The challenge of a life of learning is not just to bring passion and courage to adversity, but to make yourself ready when the time to take action arrives.

Chapter 8

Prosperity: Persistence, observation, imagination, innovation

It is a kind of spiritual snobbery that makes people think they can be happy without money. —Albert Camus

Financial success is simple. Saying it's simple doesn't mean it's easy. Nothing worthwhile is easy, and, in our culture obsessed with possessions, the hardest part seems to be building and using wealth in a humane and respectful fashion. But creating wealth is not a mystery, and it does not require any rare innate characteristics. Millions of people build wealth using down-to-earth techniques: persistence, observation, long-term commitment, and imagination.

I used all of those in one of my favorite achievements. The key was a "problem" that looked like an opportunity to me.

The Cache la Poudre River arises in the Front Range of the Rocky Mountains one hundred miles west of Fort Collins. Born in snowy peaks, it experiences minor flooding every spring when the snow melts, and occasionally roars out of its banks when a summer thunderstorm dumps a sudden downpour in the mountains. That's why zoning codes restrict building in low-lying ground that can be inundated—the floodplain.

In 1980, I wanted to buy seventeen acres of land next to the Poudre at the edge of Fort Collins. It was nice, level ground, adjacent to a major arterial leading into the city, with Interstate highway access just a few miles away. We had paid off the note to Butler, and I had some excess cash flow; the land would make a great home for a new Neenan Company headquarters. The property had mature native trees, ponds left over from its long-ago use as a gravel pit, a view of the mountains, lots of wildlife—and it was mostly in the floodplain. According to hydrologists, at least once every five centuries it would be completely awash in Poudre River floodwaters.

What on earth was I thinking?

This parcel, which we called Seven Lakes, was considered undevelopable by most people. They saw waste ground. But I used a different framework to see it as an office park, and I had an idea to mitigate the flood hazard. Why not channelize the creek that ran through it, move the resulting dirt to raise the building pads for the facilities sufficiently (three or four feet) to lift the actual development above the 500-year floodplain elevation, and thus be able to withstand a 500-year-flood if it did happen?

People scoffed.

"David, if this is such a great idea, why hasn't anybody ever thought of it before?" asked one of our bankers when he declined to help finance it. Other finance professionals had the same reaction; land use planners were skeptical, even though we prepared engineering studies to show it would work.

By this point in my life, I had become aware of the negative reaction that almost always greets new ideas, which are called *lateral thoughts*. It's a universal and understandable, if unthinking, aspect of human nature. As Woody Allen says, "I wonder who ate the first oyster?" No doubt the first proto-human who wanted to come down from the trees, the first who wanted to cook a mastodon steak, the first who wanted to sow wheat seeds—all were undoubtedly told: "If that's such a great idea, why hasn't anyone done it before?"

No one could make economic use of the Seven Lakes property until my idea helped change the community's paradigm about floodplain development. I managed to convince city officials it was workable, and I found someone very willing to finance our purchase of the property—the seller. His interest was not only financial, it was personal. "I want someone responsible on this note," he told me, "because I'll probably die before it's paid off [he was eighty], and my daughters will be getting the money."

In the end, we built eight facilities at Seven Lakes, creating work for The Neenan Company as well as making the development profitable. I dedicated the land closest to the river to a greenbelt, which includes a very popular recreation trail. The Neenan Company headquarters is at the far eastern end of the property, and my idea added considerable value to the community. When I use the greenbelt trail for a morning bike ride, like thousands of other residents, I'm benefiting from my willingness to see a problem as an opportunity, and my persistence to carry that out.

At Seven Lakes I had applied both innovative and entrepreneurial skills, and it's important to understand the difference. My new approach to floodplain development was innovative; my dedication to succeeding with it was entrepreneurial.

Creating an entirely new enterprise requires both skills, and it is a demanding task. You cannot accomplish it from your couch, at your leisure, disaffectedly. If you hear someone say that something can be done in your spare time, with little effort or risk, they are almost certainly trying to sell you a win-or-lose scheme in which (surprise!) they pocket the price of admission.

Building wealth with integrity requires passion and dedication. If you want to pursue a lateral thought you'll have to deal with naysayers. Long-term accumulation means you'll have to practice self-discipline—for decades. If you are going to rely on persistence, you'll hear "no" dozens or hundreds of times, like the creator of the copy machine did until he knocked on the door of a small firm called Xerox. My first tangible asset, the pair of shoes I bought at age twelve, came as a result of knocking on hundreds of doors to sell newspaper subscriptions. Believe it or not, I was passionately dedicated to that simple act, selling subscriptions. If you approach wealth creation with middling commitment, you'll get middling results.

There are some tested ideas and techniques that can enable wealth creation, and I've made use of all of them. Entire books have covered these topics—dozens of books, in some cases—but here's a brief overview.

Lateral Thinking

A lateral thought is an innovation that takes an entirely new tack to solving a problem. Usually, but not always, it is spurred by an obstacle, such as the once-in-five-hundred-years flood susceptibility of the ground I bought for Seven Lakes. Virtually all major human enterprises have grown and benefited from lateral thinking, ever since an early human borrowed a piece of wood on fire from a lightning strike, used the fire for warmth and food preparation, and thus inaugurated the cooking, food processing, utility, heating, and firewood industries. Her compatriots thought fire was a danger; she thought it could be a tool.

The Wright brothers solved the problem of flight—creating sufficient lift—by using a lateral thought. They already knew how to shape a wing; the real breakthrough came when they realized that the propeller also needed to be, in aerodynamic terms, a wing.

Lateral thoughts can change entire systems. Peruvian economist Hernando de Soto believes billions of "poor" people around the world can have their lives transformed by giving them documented title to what they already own—land, livestock, houses—thus creating collateral they can use as leverage to obtain credit.

Microfinance visionary Mohammad Yunus founded the Grameen Bank to make very small loans to Third World entrepreneurs—twenty dollars, say, to buy a cell phone and open a village telecommunications service. Yunus won the Nobel Prize, and he and de Soto are revolutionizing economic development by changing the paradigms of wealth and finance. You can imagine what traditional financiers told Yunus when he said he was going to found a bank that would make twenty-dollar loans to women in poor villages.

The greatest impediment to lateral thinking is not that others scoff, but that we tell ourselves it's impossible. *How can I possibly propose this? People will laugh. I must be wrong. It's changing the rules.*

Remember: If you create a new paradigm, you *are* changing the rules.

Although lateral thoughts are the basis for new enterprise, it's important to keep in mind that they often can benefit—and should benefit—human life. Pet Rocks were a huge financial success and certainly shifted the Christmas gift paradigm, but what good did that do for the world? My Seven Lakes lateral thought earned us the right to pursue a profitable office park development, and it brought the community a greenbelt and lovely stretch of recreational trail at no cost to taxpayers.

Niches

A niche is a pocket of opportunity that can make you a comfortable living, such as a restaurant, a building supply company, or a direct sales operation. Some niches can grow big enough to make you a fortune, gourmet coffee being a notable recent example. Good niches don't compete directly with the giants in an industry; if you set out to start a software company now, would you make operating-system software like Microsoft's? Niches are the launching platforms for entrepreneurs; recognizing a new and unique niche is a lateral thought.

Most of today's business giants started out in niches. Ted Turner found a television-programming niche in between CBS, NBC, and ABC—first with his "super-station" WTBS; then with the TBS cable channel; and, finally, with CNN, which has become one of the most visible businesses in the world.

Steve Jobs founded Apple Computers, because IBM, the computing behemoth of the day, wasn't making personal computers. IBM got into the business as soon as it recognized that Jobs had found a worthwhile niche. Then Michael Dell found another niche in the computer business by outsourcing manufacture of PCs and driving down the price. Now, IBM no longer makes personal computers.

A niche can simply be a new approach to an existing business. The Neenan Company's niche in the commercial construction industry, which we call Archistruction™, combines refinements of architecture, engineering, finance, land development, construction, and customer service. Believe me, it requires commitment to create a new niche in the construction industry.

Leverage

This is one of the most common and important principles of the universe, from playground teeter-totters to compound interest. It applies to business, personal finance, engineering, physics, biology—you name it, leverage is involved.

A lever is just a device or technique with which you increase or transmit effort; it's a tool that creates a mechanical advantage. Virtually all business uses some sort of leverage: Utilities leverage power over distance with transmission lines. Authors leverage a collection of words, descriptions, and ideas to millions of readers through the printed page (and now Kindles). Compound interest leverages money into more money over time. Debt instruments leverage future revenues into money to pay current costs. Restaurateurs leverage culinary achievement by opening new restaurants, selling franchises, syndicating TV shows, packaging prepped foods, or writing books. Think what you will of Wolfgang Puck, he has brilliantly used all the above to make his fortune.

Leverage is what you use to transform a lateral thought and its niche into a larger business. When you visit a banker for a loan and get it, that's leverage. So was the note I signed that enabled our purchase of the Seven Lakes property. Hiring employees is leverage: How many buildings has Donald Trump himself built? None. Me? None. Corporate mergers are leverage; so are spin-offs.

Understanding and using leverage is essential to business. And, like the seesaw in the corner playground, you have to use it correctly. Not enough, you'll stagnate. Too much, you're overextended, as The Neenan Company was in Casper, Wyoming. Artisans and creative sorts can work a niche by themselves to make a comfortable living, but that's rarely the path to wealth. Even a radical such as Andy Warhol used leverage, creating artwork designs that could be made by students and carry his imprimatur. Glass artist Dale Chihuly does the same thing today.

Most people are under-leveraged—in business. In personal life, the average American today carries so much credit card debt that government regulators were recently forced to raise the monthly minimum payment so people could pay it off in their lifetime! For the individual, that's over-leveraged. For the banks—yep, that's business leverage.

An entire society can be over-leveraged. Remember the burst U.S. housing bubble of 2008? Leverage magnifies force for good or ill; you can whistle your way right past zero without stopping. It's everywhere. Use it effectively.

Lag

You don't have to come up with a lateral thought to create wealth—you can borrow someone else's new idea that hasn't yet reached your neighborhood. The Bible says there is nothing new under the sun. Most business and creative successes represent some degree of borrowing from someone else, since worthwhile ideas don't spread throughout the human universe instantly. The time it takes for them to do so is called *lag*, and sometimes it involves decades. *Rent*, for instance, the hugely popular Broadway show and movie, is simply Puccini's opera La Boheme reconfigured with rock music. Southwest Airlines' discount air travel business model was adapted in Europe in the nineties by Ryanair—now the leader in its market—and, during the new millennium, by SpiceAir of India. How many coffee chains have borrowed the Starbucks idea? In the unlikely event that you live somewhere there isn't a local coffee roaster, you can try that idea yourself.

Where do you find lateral thoughts? Certain places are famed for their willingness to embrace new products and services, usually on continental coasts where there's considerable interaction with other cultures. California is the famous U.S. example; in China, it's Hong Kong and Shanghai.

California, for instance, is where waterbeds, skateboards, and gourmet coffee got their start. In 1971, three Seattle college graduates were looking for a business idea; one remembered a small coffee shop in Berkeley, and two of the three apprenticed with its founder, Alfred Peet. Then they returned to Seattle and opened their own coffee shop, which they called Starbucks. Imagine if you had done that! You'd have the wealth issue taken care of.

But that's just a small part of the existential challenge of leading a worthwhile life. What on earth is meaningful about wealth creation? The vast majority of human beings see it as a brutish, self-aggrandizing activity that leaves broken competitors in its wake. Most people resent those who possess wealth, as if the wealthy have no right to their prosperity—while, ironically, they believe everyone has the right to *want* wealth. Wealth creation ought to be a productive enterprise that makes many lives better, from the children for whom you can provide a good home and quality education, to the people whose work leverages your enterprise and provides their own livelihood. It's not, however, an end in itself. If dollars are all you have, you'll prove Andrew Carnegie's epithet that no one is more "pitifully wretched" than those who have only money.

The most important thing to keep in mind about wealth is that it's a tool for achieving more meaningful goals. Make sure you and your family are safe from poverty—that's pretty meaningful—and then, please, look for a way to make the world a better place. No one remembers Andrew Carnegie because he became the richest man on earth. His legacy endures because he gave his fortune away, building libraries around North America that still stand today. Bill Gates built an incomprehensible fortune—greater wealth than many small countries—and he is dedicating it to eradicating disease and improving education around the world. His example proved so powerful that the second-wealthiest individual on earth, Warren Buffet, decided to pass on his fortune to the Gates Foundation. All these people, and many others like them, have achieved a sort of wealth infinitely greater than any dollar figure. It's the satisfaction of making human life better.

Chapter 9

Patience: Wealth is accumulation, not compensation

An ounce of patience is worth a pound of brains.
—Dutch proverb

We live in a society far too focused on how many dollars people get in their weekly paychecks and, in the Wall Street corollary, on quarterly earnings reports. Once a year, *Parade* magazine produces an avidly read issue that catalogs the salaries of hundreds of Americans, from part-time child-care workers to movie stars and athletes. Every three months, stock analysts await earnings figures from corporations whose strategic timelines ought to encompass decades—and share prices can plummet or soar on the basis of a 3-percent swing, regardless of whether the company's long-term prospects are good or bad.

Compensation is important, and it's crucial for a company to show a profit. But on a short-term basis, these figures serve instant gratification rather than long-term achievement, and achieving prosperity is a long-term task. Accumulation is what builds wealth.

One of the keys to wealth accumulation is incredibly simple: Spend less than you earn. That's how Sharon and I managed to set aside enough to support buying Burton Builders, which became The Neenan Company. I was a construction cost analyst. Sharon was a schoolteacher. Neither job is particularly well-paid, but if you keep your expenses minimal, a couple can build up a so-called nest egg fairly effectively. Sharon's principle is: spend 90 percent of whatever you make. In the four years prior to our purchase of the Fort Collins construction company, we saved 50 percent or more.

This was while we were living in Kansas City in the early seventies. Our annual income was, at best, $20,000—and we lived on $6,000. Everything else, after taxes, went into the bank. Sharon sewed most of our clothes. (She still sews!) I drove a $200 car that I had to start by raising the hood and spraying the carburetor with a can of ether, keeping a fire extinguisher handy in case of explosion. Looking back, it was fun to be frugal. We knew how important saving money was for our ability to control our destiny. Money's only a tool, but in our society it's an important one.

Saving also represents another characteristic that's key to a successful and productive life. Remember that term, instant gratification? Those who can do without it achieve more. Researchers have tested this with kids. Sitting them down in a room, developmental psychologists offered them a choice between one marshmallow right away—or two later. The kids who chose the deferred reward invariably did better in school.

The other key principle to wealth accumulation is also simple. Once you have an interest in some investment instrument, let it be. Or, as they say in the casino: Let it ride. Over time, if it's any sort of growth vehicle, it will burgeon to an astounding sum.

Albert Einstein supposedly called compound interest the most powerful force in the universe. That's simplistic, but important nonetheless. If you put $10,000 in an investment account that reinvests the proceeds and grows at 10 percent a year, after thirty-three years you'll have $232,000. So, all you need do to be a millionaire in your fifties is to make that $10,000 investment four times during your twenties. Ten percent is a rare return these days, so let's put $10,000 in an investment vehicle five times in your twenties. Need a more gradual vehicle? Put $1,000 a month in an account earning 8 percent a year; start when you're twenty-five, and you can cash out at age fifty with $1.3 million.

Another example illustrates an equally important point. Start at twenty-three, by which age most Americans have finished college and begun work; put $3,000 a year into a Roth IRA that earns 8 percent, and at sixty-five you'll have $985,749. But your contribution was just $126,000, so other people have given you, in interest paid and equity appreciation, $859,749. This is worth repeating: You have gained, simply by waiting, the better part of a million dollars from other people. And you don't owe any income tax. Talk about easy money! Nonetheless, barely a tenth of American households have a Roth IRA.

It's not really easy, of course. You'd think, in modern America, that living without a $5,000 big-screen TV is extreme cultural deprivation. No SUV? Sad. These principles are the ones identified by Thomas Stanley and William Danko in their book *The Millionaire Next Door*. There are four million American households with a net worth over one million dollars, and the key strategy Stanley and Danko identified among most of them is that they built a cache of money by not spending it. They do not lease fancy cars; they live in moderate houses with modest mortgage payments; they are business owners who operate welding shops, dry cleaners, and subcontracting enterprises. Far more than half are self-employed. On average, roughly one-quarter of their wealth is in securities, one-quarter in their businesses. Virtually all are homeowners, and more than half have lived in their homes longer than twenty years. Most of these characteristics apply to me and Sharon, by the way.

Stanley and Danko also discovered that the consumer indulgences most Americans see as the trappings of wealth, such as those shiny red Porsches, are shunned by these real millionaires. "Big hat, no cattle," is the saying in Texas for those who look and act wealthy but are short on real assets. Sharon and I have a three-car garage (small by today's standards) with just two cars in it.

One other key: Investing only in one financial arena is foolish. What if your company's stock collapses? What if the stock market collapses? The whole economy? Too many American employees have watched their workplace retirement plans vaporize along with the company, as in the case of Enron, or the whole stock market during the 2008 meltdown. It's not easy to set aside savings beyond a corporate 401K, but then building wealth isn't easy.

Although I personally abhor investing in the stock market, Sharon doesn't share this aversion. She had contributed about $1,400 of her own money to our original purchase of The Neenan Company, and, about ten years later, I paid it back, figuring in a reasonable return for the use of the money. She has since taken that $14,000, invested it patiently in the stock market, and built it to about $700,000 over the intervening twenty-five years. Not bad for someone who considers it a hobby!

Most Americans practice these principles inadvertently, by buying a house in a growth market, and watching what at first seems like a daunting investment—10 percent down and a regular monthly payment—balloon into a very valuable property. Of course, you have to sell or re-mortgage your own home to cash out.

And you have to be prepared to weather down markets, such as the 2008 real estate slump that left many over-leveraged homebuyers facing foreclosure.

Despite the reality of down markets, investing in real estate is an excellent way to build wealth. Sharon and I have done so in California, without even really intending to.

To me, California truly is the Golden State. I spent many happy weeks there as a boy, visiting relatives in Santa Monica during summer vacations. So, when one of our daughters wound up at college in the San Diego area, we decided to look for property in the Del Mar district north of the city. We were visiting during parents' weekend, and asked a Realtor to take us around for a day.

We found a decent condo—one window had an ocean view—listed at $300,000. We wanted to offer $245,000. The Realtor said that wasn't nearly enough, but we persisted, and the owner countered at $247,500. That condo, which we did buy, is worth $700,000 today.

A while later, another daughter headed to school at San Diego, and we decided to find a place big enough for both girls. Another day of searching found a "fixer" listed at $180,000; we paid $168,000, invested another $32,000 in repairs, and Lindsay and Samantha lived in it throughout their college years. After that, we continued to rent it to their roommates, finally selling it in 2006 just before the California home-price bubble burst. Our net profit came to more than $300,000.

Last, but certainly not least, is the dream-getaway house we bought on a cliff overlooking the Pacific in Del Mar. We've put about $4 million into that; it's now worth, despite the real estate slump, at least $7 million. So the grand total of our property ventures in California is that we've put about $4.3 million into assets currently worth about $9 million, thus boosting our net worth almost $5 million. And all because one of our daughters went off to college.

It's the same story with almost all our ventures. I've grown my investments in The Neenan Company, an asbestos removal business, property development, banking, and several other ventures into a net worth that has made me a millionaire many times over. None of those brought anything like an overnight return; most took years, including the payback on Seven Lakes, my lateral thought. I was broke in my mid-thirties, but had managed to make my first million by the time I was forty-one.

The principles of wealth creation are inexorable. No matter how you distribute your assets, the key is not just making money— it's *keeping* money.

To that brisk axiom, I'd add that the process of patient investing engenders, within those of us who practice it, a seasoned respect for the rhythms of life and business that utterly escapes the "lucky" few who achieve wealth quickly. Patient accumulation is not luck at all, but rather faith and participation in what Camus calls the "implacable grandeur" of this life. Watching value roll upward is the real wealth, and I'm mindful of it every evening that I watch the sun set over the cresting Pacific swells I see from my balcony in Del Mar.

Chapter 10

Perturbation: Make change your ally

Change is the law of life. —John F. Kennedy

Nothing is eternal—not even taxes; and who knows about death? When The Neenan Company rose from the rubble of the Casper disaster in 1977, it was not the end of business struggle for us. Less than thirty years later, trouble returned, this time because I had made a poor decision about company leadership and let my own commitment to it get sidetracked. It became one more chance to embrace change.

Our business was in deep trouble—sales were down, morale had plunged, and we had lost more than a million dollars in the first quarter of 2004. I returned to the company after a "sabbatical" to try to lead it back to profitability and growth. We found that it was necessary to change our approach to the commercial construction business and to our customers.

One answer came in the backyard of a key salesman. Don Weidinger, one of our best business development reps, shared a property line with a neighbor who was an architect. The latter had been involved in two failed attempts by the school district in Cheyenne Wells, Colorado, to build a new school. Both times the district's voters rejected $10 million bond issues to finance the schools. The district lost $40,000 on useless design fees.

Although The Neenan Company's problems were multifaceted, one thing was sure: We needed work to help solve them. This was a classic example of the old adage that every problem is also an opportunity. The Cheyenne Wells School District wanted—and desperately needed—a new building. The Neenan Company wanted and needed new projects, and we had experience with school buildings. Could we collaborate?

Cheyenne Wells was understandably leery about yet another bond issue, so we proposed a radical approach—a change in the paradigm for such projects. Neenan Company personnel would convene a design work session with school officials and community members. We'd listen to their needs and concerns, including the deeper human concerns every building project entails, such as community identity, fiscal efficiency, and client appreciation.

The end result was what we call our "Conditions of Satisfaction," a compilation of what the community told us they wanted. We came back in a month with a design based on that. Just as important, we offered a guaranteed budget, an ironclad schedule, a more economical building (only $7 million) that was larger and served more community functions, and a promise to help the school district pass the necessary bond issue.

If the bond failed, the district would owe us nothing.

That's what is known as a transformational offer, the highest level in today's hierarchy of values. In the twenty-first century, what businesses offer customers falls within a spectrum called the Value Hierarchy that goes thus:

Transformation
Experience
Service
Product
Commodity

The higher up the list toward transformation, the greater the value. Have you noticed what people pay for weddings these days?

The lower down the list, the lesser the unit value. Compare weddings to airplane seats, which used to be luxuries but have been commoditized into bus benches.

At the bottom of the hierarchy, commodities are items in which customers have a wide range of choices, are knowledgeable about the market and can utilize alternative sources of supply. Corn, coffee, hamburgers, phone service, semiconductor chips, sugar, airplane seats, hotel rooms—all are commodities. If you want to produce something in a commodity market, you'd better be the low-cost producer, and you'd better have great skill at managing extremely slim margins and forecasting supply and demand. If you want to avoid having your business commoditized, you'd best maintain—even increase—the value that differentiates what you're offering.

The hospitality industry offers a good window to view the value hierarchy. At the bottom of the ladder are standard roadside motel rooms which are largely commodities, fluctuating between ridiculously cheap ($29.99) and moderate prices, according to traffic and season. At the other end of the spectrum are the one hundred or so resorts around the world that offer utter privacy, round-the-clock service on demand, custom menus, and matchless surroundings—such as the private island beach villa at which my coauthor spent his honeymoon in 2005. Eric and his wife spent more than $1,200 a night and considered it well-spent. It was a transformational experience that will provide a lifetime memory.

The value equation operates even at the lowest levels. Remember when you had to stay at a five-star hotel to find a fluffy terrycloth robe in your closet and a phone in the bathroom? Today they're in Holiday Inns. So, some of the ingredients of a transformational vacation have migrated all the way down the value hierarchy. And, in the never-ending search for differentiation, upper-end hotels are taking phones out of bathrooms.

Businesses that want to position themselves at the top of the hierarchy make an offer called "risk reversal"—if the experience isn't transformational, there's no charge. That was our approach in Cheyenne Wells: The school district would owe us nothing if the bond issue did not pass. We were offering an experience—a risk-free chance to improve the community—as well as a building.

The bond passed by a very slim margin, 359 to 352, but no one wanted to pay the cost of conducting a recount. We started building, and both our own spirits and the community's began to improve.

"You guys are saving our town," the mayor told our project leader when it was 30 percent complete.

"Well, you guys are saving our company," he replied.

We finished the building on time, within budget, and even brought Cheyenne Wells $300,000 in government funds by designing the gym to serve as a tornado shelter. Our project manager was declared Mayor-for-a-Day, and the assistant construction superintendent became a coach on the local high school football team, which went to the state playoffs for the first time ever. Kind of like a movie script, yes?

The Cheyenne Wells project had many positive results for everyone involved. Sociological studies have shown that, in rural areas, school decline brings community decay; when the schools close, the community dies. In Cheyenne Wells, the partnership with The Neenan Company helped save the community.

For us, building a profitable project was just the start. We gained high visibility within the rural schools community and developed close ties to school executives throughout the state. Don Weidinger attends rural schools conventions, and we have since built three dozen such projects that add up to more than $150 million. We changed the scope and profile of our business—not that we abandoned our earlier focus on high-tech and health care buildings—and I like to think we changed the atmosphere for new school projects in the rural West.

Bucky Fuller talks about the phenomenon of "emergence by emergency"—the fact that productive change seems to come about as a result of trouble, and usually just in the nick of time. If change came earlier, from a biological systems perspective, it would be waste. The Neenan Company's experiences in 1976 and 2004 demonstrate this; in each case true change was preceded by large financial losses.

This phenomenon, perturbation (which we described in Chapter 4) is the key to change—biologically, sociologically, economically, evolutionarily, even cosmologically (supernovas are preceded by perturbation within a star). If there's no disturbance to natural systems, natural creatures, and their cultures, there's no catalyst for anything new. Human beings and their systems tend to want to create order and stability. Imagine a life where you did something different each day, in a different place, with different people. But the universe is naturally disorderly and chaotic, so tiny perturbations build up until they unbalance the order and create disruption. The British colonial system was more or less stable for two centuries until the perturbations built sufficiently that the American colonists began a revolution. Our democratic republic emerged in that emergency.

There are two basic kinds of change in the universe:

- Cyclical change: The river outside the Neenan Company headquarters, the Poudre, runs high every year in spring and early summer, then starts dropping until it reaches a low in late autumn and early winter. This is a natural cycle; the spring highs and autumn lows vary from year to year, but the cyclical nature of it is steady. Notice a key characteristic: little or no perturbation.

  Oil prices, dress hemlines, interest rates, unemployment rates, inflation, rabbit populations, housing prices—all these are subject to cyclical changes in value. You can't predict exactly how high or low the value will go, or when, but you can be sure it will go up and then down again.

- Structural change: This occurs when perturbation within a system reaches sufficient volume that a breakthrough creates a new paradigm. Remember telegrams? For more than a century, the telegraph business was subject to cyclical economic factors. Then fax technology, followed by the Internet, made telegrams obsolete; and, in early 2006, Western Union sent its last telegram.

That was a structural change. Structural change is often precipitated by lateral thinking, such as when Columbus headed west in search of the Near East. The important thing to understand is that, when a structural change takes place, individuals have no option but to accept and understand it. "Roadkill" is a term for those who stand in the way of structural change. You can object to the Internet and Twitter all you like, but if you want to get a message from Poughkeepsie to San Francisco, you can no longer send a telegram. If you recently bought stock in a telegraph equipment maker...too bad.

I had tried to lead The Neenan Company to embrace change, so, in 2004, we were fairly well suited to transform our approach to business. But we had no choice: The environment for business relationships had changed, and the value customers place on work is now determined by factors my uncle Bill never had to consider while running a successful construction company in Kansas City. I imagine he'd blanch at the notion of a no-charge building proposal ("It's the pioneers that take the arrows!" is one of his favorite expressions), but the trouble that led to that proposal catalyzed new success for The Neenan Company.

I didn't like discovering that The Neenan Company was in deep turmoil once again in 2004, but this time around, the path ahead looked a bit more like an old friend and less like an enemy. The changes we made reflected changes bubbling up in society at large, and that's what keeps a company and its people young.

When you hear that change is the only constant, most people mean it's a problem. "Just when I think I have learned how to live, life changes," grumbled essayist Hugh Prather. Sea squirts are trying to avoid change of all sorts when they attach their holdfast to a rock. Resisting change is a common paradigm, but change is necessary (what's a sea squirt to do when his particular bay becomes polluted?), life-affirming, beneficial, and powerful.

So perturbation is a gift. When it hits, just ask yourself: What can I do to change my life? It's our opportunity to embrace the laws of evolution that guide life—to avoid excuses and ride the exhilarating tides of the universe.

Chapter 11

Human Dynamics: Communication is the response you get

It was impossible to get a conversation going, everybody was talking too much. —Yogi Berra

All I wanted to do was turn American education upside down, apply progressive learning theory, and make public schooling in Fort Collins a transformational experience. That's just what I said, too. How come the most important people I was talking to heard me say I wanted to turn their lives into hell?

One of the most challenging paradoxes I've discovered in life is this simple thought: Communication is the response you get.

My most painful example of this lesson came when I served as the president of the Fort Collins school board in the late seventies and early eighties. This adventure was born of a desire to help an institution that was central to my life. I had three daughters in various stages of education; The Neenan Company was hiring graduates of the system for our work crews; the overall well-being of the community in which I lived and did business relied on good education. In the end, I got more education than anyone else.

In my first four years as president, I made ever-more vigorous requests that the district stop accepting mediocrity in our educational system, and I challenged everyone involved—parents, teachers, administrators, and students—to do better. After four years, frustrated by the lack of results, I convinced the board to set a goal that would win the school district a Nobel Prize, a metaphor for aiming to reach the moon in education.

Specifically, I proposed making teachers accountable for the literacy of their students. We believed that literacy is liberation and set a goal of 100 percent literacy in five years. That doesn't seem outrageous, does it? In a prosperous, growing American community—a college town to boot—a public school district should achieve 100 percent literacy. All its students should be able to read. It sounds simple, but it's not.

I thought the answer was to aim technology and theory at the problem. That's what I was learning at the time as I expanded my own personal and business horizons—I was discovering "superlearning" techniques on my adventures in personal growth while watching prehistoric learning techniques in action in our schools. But a school district is not a business, it's a bureaucracy, and, in a bureaucracy, power belongs to the occupants, not the clients or constituents. I managed to get the support of parent groups, student groups, community groups, and the local daily newspaper, but the most important group hewed the other way. The teachers union went ballistic when it realized the literacy goal would require lots of hard work and significant change in teaching techniques—and that they would be held accountable for the success or failure of their pupils.

When you can't stand the message, attack the messenger. I had made myself into Public Enemy Number 1. The teachers called for my resignation and talked the newspaper into echoing that. A local fundamentalist church gave me an affidavit, signed by 550 people, claiming my techniques represented neo-Nazi thought and that I was the Antichrist. Those in the community who hated me were only about 20 percent, but they were a strident minority; my tires were slashed at back-to-school night.

I had actually thought I was offering ideas my new opponents would welcome. If you provide incentives for excellence, aren't you creating an environment for individuals to enhance their lives?

I believed so, but the teachers and administrators felt I was imposing orders rather than offering opportunities. I had failed to enlist them in the mission, had not convinced them of the desirability of change. This is not to excuse these "professionals" who chose to act like ostriches, but this book is about my experiences. I decided the district and its personnel were stuck in stagnation, and resigned myself to the "fact" nothing was going to change. Instead, I set about changing myself and my understanding of the world, and have endeavored to assimilate those lessons in my business and personal life.

The school board experience greatly refined my understanding of human communication—and the blocks that impair it—on both sides. Getting your message across requires courage, charisma, and clarity, and it's way more difficult than people think. What I brought to the school board was naive: Let's set some lofty goals, introduce superlearning techniques, and we'll change everything. But answers to complex problems are not so simple, and imposing huge challenges on other people requires leadership for which my skills were not sufficient in that place and time.

How can I be responsible for what other people take from my communication? Not only does that challenge seem impossible, it looks intrusive—I am my own person declaring my own truth on my individual path. Isn't it simply my job to put information out there, and other people can exercise free will and take whatever they like from it? In fact, taking responsibility for communication is both powerful and pragmatic. You can talk until you're blue in the face, but if the human being you are talking with doesn't get it, you haven't communicated.

We're all familiar with the idea that most communication is non-verbal. Talking is simply making words out loud, presenting information. Information is important, but it's only a small part of communication. The bigger portion is what I call "essence"— your true nature, your core, the inborn character you had when you arrived in the world. Babies have it, and the process of growing up complicates it. When we're born, we depart an environment of perfect comfort and security for the cacophony and challenge of life outside the womb. Every time we are bruised or hurt, we protect that vulnerable essence; and, by the time we're adults, after hearing that barrage of 385,000 negative messages (according to child development researchers, that's the average), we are all walking around in a suit of body armor. This is nothing new. "For man has closed himself up," wrote William Blake, "till he sees all things thro' narrow chinks of his cavern."

But we can change that. Leaders who do so, who free their essence and convey it to others, have what is known as "charisma." Just imagine a convenience store clerk saying: "Ask not what your country can do for you; ask instead what you can do for your country." Now, recall John Kennedy stirring a nation with those famous words. JFK was issuing a challenge, a huge one, and he got his message across. I know, because when I heard it I signed up for the U.S. Army. I was on the University of Mississippi campus, attached to the 101st Airborne, keeping order when James Meredith, the first-ever black student, enrolled.

Since all communication is a two-way event, learning the art of real communication requires that we learn to hear as well. This happens to be a crucial aspect of accepting love and support: seeking outside perspectives about ourselves. No one can tell you your truth. But other people, especially those closest to us, have extremely valuable feedback to offer. Are you really patient enough to become a kindergarten teacher? Your spouse knows. Do I really remain respectful, even when I'm angry? The people who work for me can say. When I need an unvarnished opinion about something in my life, I often rely on Sharon.

Recovering addicts and alcoholics rely on such outside perspectives to straighten out their lives. These "sponsors" follow the longstanding custom of passing on their experience and hope to those just starting out, a relationship that benefits both participants. They practice "tough love": a sponsor tells the unvarnished truth.

My friend Bob Bender describes three levels of communication:

- Mouth-to-ear is simply words that carry information. Need directions to the hotel from the airport? Got a list of things for your husband to pick up at the store? This type of conversation has its place, but it's superficial. If this is the level at which you communicate something that challenges others, as I clearly did when I was on the school board, it will often be received as an attack.

- Thought to thought represents a deeper level, an exchange of ideas. In a philosophical debate between colleagues about which computer system to buy, both brains are engaged. Intellectual interaction takes place, but not emotional or spiritual. Once again, at this level, challenging information is often considered an attack. I debated the merits of

different educational approaches with many teachers, and
we were having thought-to-thought communication. It
availed me nothing.

- Heart-to-heart communication takes place when each
individual's essence comes into play. Bender says when
it happens you can feel it on both sides, and that's exactly
right. This is the level of communication essential to
conveying a challenge to others. If you achieve it, you are
making a transformational offer.

Uncovering and revealing your essence is a vast personal
enterprise in which many people invest years and, in the case of
psychotherapy, huge amounts of money. Suffice it to say that the
more willing you are to risk exposing your real self to someone
else, the more likely they are to free their own. It's one more
paradox: The more you give away, the more you will get.

Communicating your essence does not mean unleashing raw
anger and aiming it at someone else like a gun. The rules of human
courtesy apply. And if you are compelled to offer a challenge
to someone, it's usually best to ask permission beforehand.
Imposition of challenge—intervention—is justified only when a
problem is severe: for instance, when your husband has just been
arrested for drunk driving.

At The Neenan Company, we endeavor to follow the rules
of verbal interaction propounded by Ben Franklin and Native
American medicine man Rolling Thunder.

- Speak with good purpose; if it does not serve, do not say it.
- When you disagree or do not understand, ask clarifying
questions.

I'm not saying these principles should be the foundation of all interactions. Such "good" communication, as Harvard business theorist Chris Argyris wryly calls it, is unlikely to produce any of the perturbation that leads to learning and growth. But it's up to each individual to decide when he or she is ready to have a learning experience. Good leaders use their essence to inspire others to make exactly that decision.

As for public education—sometimes you just cannot get your message across. I didn't, and I haven't been tempted since to seek public office. The illiteracy rate in our local school district is now approaching 30 percent. If all those kids can't read and write, how well do you think they communicate?

Chapter 12

Love: I now allow others to love and support me

Everything that lives, lives not alone, nor for itself.
—William Blake

The last time I saw my dad was early July, 1961, in Kansas City. He and my brothers Peter, Ted, Mark, and Guy were headed west to visit my grandparents in California. They made a quick stop in Kansas City to see me and pick up a station wagon from my Uncle Jimmy. I was eighteen and working that summer for another uncle, Bill Clarkson, whom I later went to work for full-time. I was a carpenter's helper on the 12th Street viaduct project, making three dollars an hour, excellent pay at the time. It was one of the best times of my life. I'd hated school; here I was making good money in KC, had my own apartment, was on my own. I loved it. So when my dad and four brothers stopped by, I shook my dad's hand—the only time I ever did so—and wished them all a good trip.

A week later, outside Reno, Nevada, Dad was tired, and, at 2:00 AM, turned the wheel of the car over to Peter, who was fifteen and didn't have a driver's license. Something went wrong, the car went off the road and rolled, and in the accident my dad received a basal skull fracture. The four boys got dings and bruises and a few broken bones, but were otherwise okay.

My uncle Jimmy called and said something bad had happened, could I please come to his house. By the time I got there and walked into the dining room, he'd received a second call from Nevada. "David, I'm afraid the worst has happened. Your dad died this morning." I was stunned.

"You have to be the responsible one now," Jimmy continued. "Your mother isn't up to handling this herself. So you'll have to go to Reno and bring your brothers and your dad's body home." And he gave me a handful of $100 bills.

So many of us grow up with the idea that we must be impenetrable pillars of strength, self-sufficient, and utterly independent. This is especially true of men, but women acquire the notion, too. Accept help? Only if there is no other option and we've already fallen halfway down the cliff. Ask for help? Never. It's a sign of weakness.

Luckily, I've had several occasions in my life when help came my way whether I asked for it or not, and I learned thereby one of the most important lessons of all. The day my dad died was the first of two occasions that my Uncle Jimmy brought the lesson home.

My dad was forty-one when he died; I was eighteen. In all those eighteen years, he had never hugged me and had, in fact, made it clear that my job was to grow up quickly and help with my brothers and sisters. When I was a boy, he taught me how to fix a flat tire on my bike the first time it happened—and then sent all my brothers to me when their bikes got flat tires. If they learned, great; if not, I had to keep working with them until they did.

Now, we would all have to rely on each other. My mother and I flew out to Reno. The whole way out there, I felt little, if any, grief. Instead, I was angry at my dad for having put Peter, an untrained driver, in control of a vehicle. The county sheriff was intending to charge my brother with manslaughter. "Sir, why don't you just let us all go home?" I asked. "I'll bring my brother back if we have to." No doubt, I managed to truly communicate my essence then. He looked me up and down. "Son, you go right ahead," he said, and dropped the charges on the spot.

My dad was lying in an open casket at the mortuary in Reno, and my mother called me over. "This is your last chance to see him. Doesn't he look peaceful?" I thought she was nuts. What about all the problems that faced us now? My mother had just given birth to my sister Claire, whom we later discovered was barely educable and would need care all of her life. And then there were my other eight siblings, all still in schools of one sort or another.

I came home from Kansas City and took a number of jobs to help support my mom and siblings. I drove a water truck, shoveled coal, worked in circulation at the newspaper—sometimes holding down two jobs at once. I was a sophomore at the University of Missouri, but I wasn't doing well in school.

Six months later, Jimmy came to visit. "David, how's life?" he asked me. I said it sucked.

"I think it's time you got on with your life, then," he continued. He told me he was going to give my mom $200 a week so she could make the house payment and cover living expenses for our very large family. She'd have to work, of course, and all my brothers and sisters would have to help out. But they'd be set for food and shelter, and I could go off and live my own life.

That year, difficult as it was, taught me how resilient I am. No matter what comes up, I can make it through. "David, I have faith in you. You'll do fine," my mother had often told me when I was a boy. When we are children, social psychologists say, we receive a hundred times more negative messages than affirmative ones; and people who wind up with serious emotional trouble in their adult lives are often the ones who receive no nurturance in their first three years. That positive endearment from my mother must have settled in my bones, because, as I grew up, I had faith in myself, too.

It taught me something even more crucial: Those who love us want to help. My uncle Jimmy saved my family and opened the door for me to start my own life.

I now allow others to love and support me. That's the lesson I have taken from moments like these. I first heard this idea from my friend and mentor Marshall Thurber, and it was revelatory: I can embrace other people and seek and accept their love and support. And I can still live an autonomous, existential life. That simple phrase has become one of my favorite personal affirmations, reminding me that I'm a member of many communities of human connection, starting with family and friends.

Yes, it seems paradoxical to the idea of taking responsibility for your own path. But it's just one glistening facet of the universe that sparkles with new color every time I look into the cosmic kaleidoscope. Paradoxes are everywhere. The fact that responsible people need love and support is just one paradox among many, and it's a particularly lovely one.

Self-sufficiency and autonomy are certainly important; mature adults call on these attributes when necessary, as I had to when my dad died. An old Swedish proverb says that the best place to find a helping hand is at the end of your own arm. But many times in life, my own hands have been inadequate to the task, and learning to ask for and accept help is key to almost any success. It's incredibly important to be open to accepting the love and support of other human beings, and, for many of us, that's far more difficult than helping ourselves. When my uncle Jimmy stepped in to support my mom, and freed me from trying to carry the whole family on my shoulders, he gave me a priceless gift of freedom and understanding. So, in that instance, accepting help made it possible for me to take responsibility for my own life.

Embracing such paradoxes helps me appreciate the infinite flavors of being alive. Understanding and welcoming paradox adds depth and richness to daily life and helps enable transformational action. Encountering a paradox usually means you are facing some higher truth.

For example, struggle is the doorway to growth and peace; problems are opportunities; freedom means taking responsibility; practice is the key to artistry—they are all paradoxes. This too is part of the makeup of the universe. Gravity is one of the weakest of forces, yet it shapes the whole cosmos. Matter and energy are intertwined and, at the level of quantum physics, seem to be both different and the same. The forces that create an orbit are opposites—gravity attracts, momentum pulls away. The orbit cannot exist without both.

Keep that in mind when you think of your relationship with your spouse. What a lovely paradox!

The paradox that shines brightest in my daily life is the fact that responsible people need love and support. In fact, it can be irresponsible not to accept it. We all know of people who face crippling trouble in life, such as drug addiction, and refuse help.

I'm the chairman of a fully integrated design-build company—but can I produce a finished building by myself? Can I sell, design, plat, finance, engineer, and construct? It would be ridiculous for me to try. True, we pay a salary to the Neenan Company employees who do design and build the building, but there is more to the transaction than a simple exchange of time and effort for money. Our employees support our goal of operating a world-class, innovative company. A number of us have been together a long time, and we offer each other a very real kind of love.

I've come to realize that people *want* to help. When I ask for and accept support from someone else, I am offering them an opportunity to feel better about themselves and to turn their energies outward. It's not just a two-way street—it's an infinite web. "Everyone needs help from everyone," said Bertolt Brecht.

There's an important difference between supporting someone and propping them up. My uncle Jimmy didn't give me $200 a week; he gave my mother an income (not a blank check) to pay living expenses and urged me to get out in the world and find my path. That's support. My best friend, John Duffy, declined to lend me money during the Casper disaster. Instead, he sat down with me and helped me identify the path to business recovery that I followed. If you aid your daughter in learning how to play softball by taking her out on the ballfield to play catch, that's support. If you coerce the Little League coach into giving your son a spot on the team, that's enabling. Support, in other words, takes place when we use our resources, time, and talents to provide the framework in which someone else learns something for themselves. If you read this book or take my course and use the ideas within to take action that transforms your life, you have accepted love and support from me.

I had the opportunity to support my co-author when he set out on the path of recovery more than two decades ago. When Eric got sober, he "woke up" to discover that he was $18,000 in debt, and creditors were lined up outside his door. He felt the situation was hopeless but asked me for advice. I encouraged him to call each creditor and arrange a repayment schedule—almost everyone in business understands this situation, I told him, and will honor an honest effort to make good. That was 1983, and I had recently worked out of a $670,000 hole, so I knew the territory. Eric didn't really believe me, frankly, but went ahead; fifteen months later he paid off his last debt.

Please notice the form that love and support took: I passed on information, experience, and encouragement. Eric took action, and thereby learned a lesson that he himself has passed on to others.

Love and support are not always free. If you take advantage of the services of a humane, experienced therapist to clear up childhood troubles, that is love and support—and believe me, it won't be free. I've done that.

One of my most effective allies has been the banker with whom I've nurtured a relationship for decades, Tom Gleason. He's the one who chose to help us rather than bail out on us during the Casper crisis in 1976. You can still find bankers like that today. People do believe that character counts, and they make decisions on that basis. Yes, Tom's bank made money on its support of The Neenan Company, as well it should.

When you have the chance to give or accept love and support, please do so with fearless passion. Keep in mind the axiom common in self-help groups that a problem shared is divided; a joy shared is magnified. Asking for support isn't shopping; giving love isn't analysis. On both sides, one of the most important vehicles for love is a huge, heartfelt hug. Paradoxically, the more often you accept this physical intimacy from someone you love, the stronger you are to stand alone. So wrap your arms around your spouse, friend, partner, or client and hold tight for a moment. I don't mean a quick, perfunctory squeeze. Just draw yourself close and really go for it. Then go sail the seas of life until the next time you have the chance to hold tight to someone you love.

Chapter 13

Partners: Your companions are your most precious assets

It is not in the stars to hold our destiny but in ourselves.
—Shakespeare

I met Sharon Wells while I was winding up my college career at the University of Missouri. It was a blind date; a friend suggested I ask her to a football game, and that was so much fun I invited her to a gathering some fraternity guys were having along the Missouri River. I spent most of the time talking to her, and, over the course of the next few months, she became my best friend.

Sharon saw me off to Australia three months later. While I was overseas, I wrote her pretty regularly—"What's this guy writing me so much for?" she wondered, since she already had a boyfriend—and she wrote back occasionally, though she made it clear she wasn't pining around Missouri hoping I would come back. Eventually, I realized what I felt was far more than friendship. I really loved her.

There's more to it than that—our cultural notions of love are cluttered up with garish distractions rooted in sex, romance, glamour, thrill, destiny. All those things have their place, but few decisions you make in life are more important than choosing mates, partners, friends, supporters, and companions—and a spouse is all those in one. This is a task that requires equal amounts intuition, emotion, and intellect. Think of it as similar to picking a partner for a difficult mountain climb, to use an analogy posed by business teacher and friend Jim Collins. You'd better pick the right partner; if you don't, and you fall, you're dead. Adventuring is great, but long-term partner selection is no time to just roll the dice. You can't learn or achieve anything if you don't survive a serious fall.

When it comes to the love part of partnership, this is not an easy task. We are genetically designed to spread our seed far and wide (both male and female); psychologists have identified specific cues that prompt biochemical changes in men and women designed to spur mating, child-rearing—and then partner-switching. Evolutionarily, the more mating diversity, the better. This is what's known as our limbic system in action.

But, if we are to let biochemistry alone guide us, we might as well be sea squirts, heedless in the ocean of life.

I'd seriously dated four other young women before Sharon; luckily, my limbic system did not provoke any sort of genetic mingling with them. My relationship with Sharon, by contrast, was rooted in my frontal lobe, where emotion and judgment live side by side, rather than in my atavistic limbic system. We began with friendship more than romance. It was clear to me that she was a very strong person; she always had an opinion and always told me what she wanted. I didn't have stars in my eyes—I had a vision of us being old, laughing together. We were married June 21, 1969.

Sharon is dynamic, sensible, acute, resilient, and healthy. She has a great sense of humor and doesn't shy away from making fun of me, herself, or anyone else. She is an independent, free spirit who stands up to me.

When our daughter Jessica was two, she misbehaved and I spanked her. Sharon told me not to do that. "But," I said, "she has to learn limits somehow." Sharon replied, "Nobody ever spanked me, and I turned out fine, didn't I?" She has been a wonderful mother to our four daughters, and she is a common sense, down-to-earth human being who offers a good counterpart to my more flamboyant personality.

For years, she has applied patience and prudence in careful stock-market investing (which I can't stand) and has built up quite a sizeable portfolio of her own.

Even though her down-to-earth nature helps keep me grounded, she is, at the same time, remarkably adventurous (another paradox). When I was finally ready to buy a business that required moving to a new city in a new state, I came home from the scouting trip and told Sharon this looked like the right opportunity in the right place.

"Great," she said. "Where?"

"Fort Collins, Colorado," I told her.

"When?" she asked.

"Well, it's almost spring—we need to go in a couple weeks," I explained.

"Well, as a teacher I can give two weeks notice. Let's go," she said, never having seen Fort Collins. And off we went.

During the Casper crisis, at the point my spirits were lowest, I was moping around the house one day and Sharon decided she'd had enough.

"How much have we lost?" she asked me.

"Hundreds of thousands more than we have," I moaned.

"And how much money did you think you would make back when you were a paperboy?"

"Millions."

"So, what's a few hundred thousand? David," she told me, "I haven't lost confidence in you. Have you lost confidence in yourself?"

I had. But Sharon's reminder helped me gain it back.

One of my old intellectual models, Bucky Fuller, used to advise: Don't fall in love. It's not *falling*. *Orbit* in love, he urged. Consider yourselves two separate planets, each with your own gravity and path, sharing a part of the universe in which you orbit around each other, independent, but with intertwining orbits. If you "fall" in love you can't tell where one person ends and the other begins. Remember how, in space, both the gravity of attraction and the impetus of separate momentum *together* are what create an orbit. Think of a loving partnership as an infinitely flexible holdfast between two spouses.

That's how Sharon and I have lived for more than four decades. Each of us has our own interests, friends, and philosophies, though we do share many values.

We are both interested in business and finance, for example. While I lead the Neenan Company, she has been a volunteer credit counselor, helping people understand how to get out of financial trouble. I'm an avid bike rider; she likes to skate, dance, and play golf. She invests in the stock market; I invest in real estate, startup businesses, and, of course, have built The Neenan Company for forty years. Meanwhile, she runs the household budgets, and she helps manage the "Business & You" operations. We have separate bank, credit, and investment accounts; and we have joint accounts. We travel together, and we travel individually, too.

Sharon has always supported me, never lost confidence in me, and that has been a matchless contribution to my life. We've been orbiting each other for most of our lives, and the balance remains as strong as ever. I can think of no more important asset in my life.

Chapter 14

Precession: In search of the great Perhaps

Nothing happens without personal transformation.
—W. Edwards Deming

Although I always knew I would create wealth and run a business, I never intended to become a personal growth "teacher." All I wanted to do after the Casper disaster back in 1976 was return The Neenan Company to profitability and transform myself into a better corporate leader. But the experience had an utterly unexpected side effect.

In the early eighties, once we had repaid our debt to Butler Manufacturing, Butler executives invited me to pass on my "secrets" to some of the company's other builders.

"Who on earth," I asked, "would want to hear what I have learned?"

"We have more than nine hundred builders, and most of them owe us money," they explained.

I put together the key points of The Neenan Company's resurrection and worked up a one-day presentation. I was reasonably accustomed to public speaking as a member of the Fort Collins School Board, and I felt I had some pretty profound ideas and techniques to pass along. I conducted a half-dozen such sessions with Butler owners, but most were simply not motivated to transform their business practices. They were older guys who'd been successful enough to have money in the bank and were ready to hit the golf course.

However, the experience introduced me to the whole world of personal growth, business philosophies, and human potential training. I had already discovered superlearning—pathbreaking information about the learning process, such as the importance of color, note-taking, and review for retention. Where, I wondered, did that come from? So I embarked on a yearlong journey into the world of personal growth and business theory. I took an avid interest in Werner Erhard, Buckminster Fuller, W. Edwards Deming, Viktor Frankl, Chris Argyris, Eric Hoffer, Fernando Flores, Fred Kofman, Peter Senge, and many others. (Please see the bibliography at the end of this book.) I walked on hot coals, screamed primally, and dangled from ropes. And I discovered a wonderful seminar that synthesized much of this, "Money & You," taught by Marshall Thurber. Marshall had been an attorney and a successful real estate developer in California, then had studied with Bucky and Deming and begun teaching the principles of success with integrity. His course was difficult, experiential, intellectually rigorous, and humane.

Something about the whole experience called to my soul. Encountering vivid new ideas, challenging myself to change, meeting radically different thinkers—I loved it all. I decided to immerse myself in Marshall's course.

My nature does not lend itself to passive, back-of-the-room participation, so I told him I wanted to learn to teach the course, too, and I began shadowing him as he taught, helping out as a staff member. I did so for fifty-five days in 1983–84 and took part in advanced instruction he was offering, called "Jedi training," designed to create new teachers of his material.

Then I began assuming responsibility for parts of Marshall's course. I began with some of the introductory role-playing games that are key to the course's experiential learning, then took over some of the more challenging parts. If they weren't challenging enough, Marshall made sure they were. At one point, I was going to lead a game called Ring Toss, designed by Harvard Business School theorists, in which participants learn about wealth creation. Marshall instructed the other would-be trainers to act rowdy, drunk, disinterested, and obstructive; and I was unable to get their attention. After a while Thurber interrupted the fiasco, invited everyone to go to lunch and "suggested" I sit there and think about what had happened. After lunch, they came back, still noisy and inattentive.

"Stop!" I roared. That got their attention.

"Okay, we all believe in free will, so I'm going to offer you characters a choice. If all you want to do is party, here's one hundred dollars"—I pulled the bills out of my pocket—"please take it and head for the bar.

"But, if you'd like to learn how to make one hundred dollars a minute, let's play this game. Your choice. Party or learn." They played. And I learned.

I also filmed Marshall teaching the course and studied that. I wrote a script for my own version and memorized it (and still consult it when I'm teaching). After eight months of this apprenticeship, I "graduated" to teach an entire course as sole instructor in Atlanta in December, 1983.

In all, I participated in more than thirty such seminars before I ever took the stage at the front of a room to teach it myself. That's market research, yes? Since then, I have led more than two hundred sessions of Business & You in ten countries and numerous languages. Marshall still does human potential training and remains an incredibly intriguing, challenging, and astute thinker, and one of my mentors. In all the years of learning I have under my belt, Marshall's teaching has been the best ever—my catalyst for accelerated learning.

Over the years I have adapted and changed the course significantly, and acquired "ownership" of the material under the name "Business & You."

Teaching "Business & You" has been central to my own growth. If you really want to learn something, you teach it. Every time I stand in front of a roomful of initially skeptical participants, I make mistakes and learn.

I've also had many simply wonderful human experiences, and gained a profoundly greater understanding of the world outside the relatively safe confines of Fort Collins. The aspirations the course covers are so universal to the human spirit that I've been able to teach B&Y in cultures that are foreign in much more than language. I've taught ethical capitalism in China. I've explained love and support in countries that have been at war for generations. I described freedom and its challenges to people who've been oppressed for centuries.

In Poland, where I first taught B&Y in 1991, our local producer told us we needed to add a word to a role-playing game in which participants communicate the essence of something. "Forgiveness," she said, "add that. We've been angry at other people for more than two hundred years." Indeed, Poland has been a pawn before the march of armies since 1756, when the entire country was erased by Austria, Prussia, and Russia. We did add forgiveness (not just in Poland), and today, when I bring B&Y to Poland, I find a dynamic people who hold few grudges and are invigorated by their place in modern Europe.

Also in the early Nineties, in Estonia, I taught the course to a roomful of stony-faced men who hardly reacted for three days—until the very end, when we all stood together, arms linked, tears streaming down our faces. "What happened?" I asked. "You guys fought me tooth and nail for three days. Now you won't leave."

"What did you expect?" one replied. "We've been slaves for 2,000 years and free for a few months."

In 1993, in Romania, we trekked to a conference center in a small village in the Carpathians. At the end of the course, the participants told us: We've never been out of Sibu, Romania. We always wondered if love exists in the outside world. It's wonderful to find that it does.

I haven't made any notable income conducting "Business & You;" in fact, I used to do the seminar for nothing, but the IRS objected, concluding it was a vehicle for me to take overseas vacations. (In Novosibirsk?) The fees I charge now pay my expenses and those of some of the staff members who help, and bring a worthwhile return to the local producers who provide the venue and logistical support.

And how can you explain this huge detour that appeared in my life, philosophically? Buckminster Fuller calls it *precession*.

The technical definition is complicated. According to Bucky, precession is "the intereffect of individually operating cosmic systems upon one another. Since Universe is an aggregate of individually operative systems, all of the intersystem effects of the Universe are precessional, and the 180-degree imposed forces usually result in redirectional resultants of 90 degrees."

That's a mouthful. Bucky also said, for lay understanding, that what he meant by precession is very similar to what most people call side effects. In other words, the choices we make and actions we take yield unanticipated results that veer from our intended direction.

For instance, twenty-five years ago, a young Fort Collins newspaper reporter was assigned to do an article about me and an investment scam by which I'd been victimized. After we talked at length, he returned to his editor and declared it was not a legitimate story. (And got in hot water as a result.) That was the beginning of my friendship with my co-author, Eric Lucas, and neither one of us could have predicted it would lead years later to this book.

Other examples are easy to think of. Columbus set off to chart a new way to the East Indies and found the Western Hemisphere. Alexander Fleming was simply studying the properties of bacteria, when he noticed that a certain mold inhibited its growth, thus "discovering" penicillin and the existence of antibiotics. John Sutter was running water through a grain mill when he noticed something golden glinting in the millrace—you can credit that for modern California.

The most important thing about precession is that it applies to bodies in motion. Stagnation does not yield precession. If you spend most of your life on the couch, unexpected marvels will not come your way.

To unleash precession in your own life, you must set yourself in motion. I started The Neenan Company to make money and secure my family's financial future; that adventure has helped in many ways to improve the social order in our home town and the many places we work. That's the real purpose of having goals, making plans, setting out on a journey—in search, as Rabelais put it, of the great Perhaps. If your vision is to start a business and create wealth for you and your family, that's great, and I hope you succeed. But what I most wish for you is that the effort will lead to some other unknown purpose or discovery that will lie at a tangent to your original goal. It is not really sheer happenstance.

Lewis Thomas, renowned science author and former president of Memorial Sloan-Kettering Cancer Center, said, "I'm not as fond of the notion of serendipity as I used to be. It seems to me now that as you get research going…things are bound to begin happening, if you've got your wits about you. You create the lucky accidents."

So who could have imagined that, during those dark days in 1976 when bankruptcy loomed and my health was marginal, that crisis would lead to my adventures around the world? I certainly couldn't. It was the furthest thing from my mind.

Suppose, after emerging from the Casper disaster fiscally sound and personally healthy, I had decided to just stay put in life and savor my success? I call that maundering over past glory, and I'd have missed a million remarkable experiences. Precession brings life's biggest delights and surprises. In this case, struggle and despair brought wonder and discovery and purpose—because I was in motion.

Chapter 15

Integrity: Principles come before profit

It is curious that physical courage should be so common in the world and moral courage so rare. —Mark Twain

Management is doing things right. Leadership is doing the right things. —Peter Drucker

One day in 1987, I received a call from a potential Neenan Company client. His name was Eddie Yabaggie, and we were among the three final candidates to build a new facility in Denver for his company, DataRay Corporation. Our proposal was a good one, but Eddie didn't have any clear preference for our services until one of his business associates visited him.

"One of my most important vendors is putting pressure on me," he told me on the phone. "He's telling me that unless I hire The Neenan Company for our new building, he won't make another part for us. I've never heard of anything like this."

Eddie's vendor was Ted Yoshida, who owned a sheet metal parts fabrication firm in Louisville, Colorado, called Kenray Corporation. We'd built a new facility for Ted almost a decade earlier, and, while the building itself was great, there'd been a small problem outside. We didn't judge the site soils correctly, and the asphalt parking lot that we recommended and installed began to fail. Within a year it showed alligator cracking, the harbinger of eventual breakdown.

Ted and I had gone to dinner about a year after his building was done, and I told him that The Neenan Company ought to fix the parking lot—but we were still recovering from the Casper disaster, and I just didn't have enough money to do so. When the money was available, I would, I promised. No doubt, he thought, *yeah, right.*

It took five more years. Kenray's parking lot was one of those nagging, incomplete things that take up residence in my conscience and occasionally wake me up at 4:00 in the morning. Sooner or later, when something is embedded that firmly in my psyche, I have to take care of it. So, in 1985, when our business was back on solid ground and we were thriving, we sent crews over to Ted's facility, tore out the asphalt and put in a brand-new, stronger, longer-lasting concrete lot.

When we were done, Ted called me up and asked how much the new concrete parking lot cost. "Fifty thousand," I told him. "How much less would an asphalt lot cost?" he asked. The difference was $20,000, and Ted sent me a check for that amount.

And two years later, he went to see Eddie Yabaggie and told Eddie he should hire us for his new building. That was one of several occasions Ted served as a fervent reference for The Neenan Company, completely of his own volition.

In effect, he was a missionary on our behalf. There is no more effective sales tool than customer testimonials, especially when they are rendered independently, as Ted was doing. Listening to and rectifying customer complaints creates profound customer loyalty—deeper loyalty, researchers find, than if the customer were simply satisfied in the first place. No one is surprised when mistakes happen, particularly experienced business people. Fixing mistakes honorably and genuinely is more rare, and more memorable, than making them in the first place.

It would have been within mainstream business practice to let Ted Yoshida's parking lot go. In ten or twenty years it would have been a mess, but those were the specs he agreed to, and, hey, stuff happens. Overall, Ted might have said he was satisfied with our work, even with a crumbling asphalt lot.

The Neenan Company departs from the mainstream as often as we can. We've replaced a metal roof that had a few dents in it; again, it wasn't a pressing problem, and would have taken years to cause trouble. We've told potential customers, after reviewing their needs and current facilities, that they don't need a new building—they need a new production system. Amazed, they tell us: When we really do need a building, we'll call you.

Replacing a parking lot five years later is radical customer service (though it shouldn't be) and the story of Ted's advocacy for our company is colorful. However, the point isn't great customer service and its rewards. I wasn't fretting about Ted's parking lot at 4:00 AM because of the potential effect on future sales. It bothered me because it wasn't right. It contravened my most important value, integrity.

Stanley Marcus, former chairman of Neiman Marcus, once discovered to his dismay that the company had sold as solid silver some household implements that were silver wash. The items were in the store's famous Christmas catalog; the chairman of Tiffany bought some, noticed they weren't real silver, and called Marcus. The latter called in the buyer responsible and asked him to explain.

"Well, he's the only one who can tell the difference," the buyer argued. "Send Tiffany a real one. No one else will know."

"Wrong," said Marcus. "I'll know. I want you to track down everyone who bought these and replace them with real ones." And so they did, for all five thousand customers.

I'm fond of a Chinese saying (probably Taoist) that declares: The long road *is* the short road. There aren't shortcuts to integrity. To an accountant, replacing a parking lot is a cost. To a smart business person, it's an investment. To a leader, it's the right thing to do.

This idea goes both ways in this story. Ted Yoshida did not need to make up the cost between asphalt and concrete when we redid his parking lot. It would have been within mainstream business practice for him to thank us and go on his way. He, too, made a decision based on his integrity. Countless times in my life I have encountered instances where integrity meant bypassing an expedient choice and making a more difficult one. Each occasion has proven the worth of that Taoist longer road.

A quarter-century ago, the world's largest brewer, Anheuser-Busch, came to my hometown in Fort Collins, Colorado, with a proposal to build a new brewery just outside the city limits. It would add hundreds of jobs, hundreds of thousands of dollars in taxes, and $500 million in capital spending to the city's economy. Naturally, the local business community embraced the idea.

There was one catch: Busch also wanted to build a coal-fired power plant for its brewery. Just twenty-two tons of sulfur dioxide a year. Surely Fort Collins wouldn't mind?

Fort Collins residents take their natural environment quite seriously. We enjoy cleaner air and water than most other economically prosperous areas, and, with the Rocky Mountains at our back and the High Plains at our doorstep, the landscape is a large part of our quality of life and economic vitality. Coal-burning doesn't fit into that. The business community faced a dilemma: We would love to welcome Busch to town, but not twenty-two tons of sulfur dioxide.

The Fort Collins Chamber of Commerce wrestled with this challenge for several months, asking its members what they thought. I argued strongly that the community would not accept the company's plan. In the end, the Chamber let Busch know it opposed the power plant idea, and the company backed down on that issue.

In effect, Fort Collins told one of the world's biggest corporations that it would have to honor our values in order to be welcomed to town. Busch could easily have chosen to start over elsewhere, and—Poof!—there go all those jobs and dollars. Any number of other cities wanted the brewery, no questions asked.

The company stuck with Fort Collins, and today Busch is a major component of the Fort Collins economy. And the community had demonstrated one of the most important principles of human life: Integrity matters.

Without integrity, success is pointless. In business and commerce, making money is important (even Trappist monks do so), but just making money is not sustainable in and of itself. There is more to life than "success." Human beings who pile up money at the expense of all else have an open hole in their soul that they are trying to fill with cash, or status, or a sports score. It doesn't work.

This is not an overly complex issue. It's not hard to recognize where integrity lies. In their book *Moral Intelligence*, Doug

Lennick and Fred Kiel say, "Integrity is authenticity. It is saying what you stand for and standing for what you say."

So, do I want to live my life pretty much straight up, or am I okay with being a scoundrel? Many people go through daily life unconscious of how their choices answer that question.

By the dictionary definition, *integrity* means, first of all, moral uprightness and honesty; and, second, wholeness and soundness. Though, technically, the second part refers to structural integrity, this is the layer of meaning that matters the most to me. I see integrity as a state in which your values and your actions are in balance.

Have I been out of integrity? Often. Remember when I was sitting in a hospital bed, smoking a cigarette and ignoring medical guidance about how to restore my health? I had three young daughters at the time, a family to support, and a company to lead that employed several hundred people. Leaders have several key tasks, and setting an appropriate example is one of the most important. (Not to mention avoiding costly, unnecessary medical bills!)

I had a moment in 2006 when I discovered I was out of integrity. I was being sued for $58 million. I'd been in business for three decades, but I had never been involved in a lawsuit before, as either plaintiff or defendant, and it was an excruciating experience. At one point during the trial, the plaintiff's lawyer developed a nosebleed. I found myself gloating over that, and was filled with hate and anger. Later, I ran into an acquaintance, a doctor who had also been sued. When I described my situation, he pointed out my obvious mental state: "I was just like you. It was terrible." I recognized I had descended into resentment, resignation, and righteousness—what I call the "toxic mental cocktail," the worst frame of mind a human being can adopt.

I had to change my mood, exercising what Viktor Frankl called the last of human freedoms—the ability to choose one's attitude. I worked on becoming calm, firm, responsible. It changed my entire experience in the rest of the trial, which ended in our favor. No $58 million judgment, no wipeout of The Neenan Company or the Neenan family.

But, I repeat, money is not the reward for integrity. It is its own reward.

Chapter 16

Values: Ideas that guide action

To succeed in life, you need three things: a wishbone, a backbone, and a funny bone. —Reba McEntire

Sharon and I weren't poor when we started our married life back in Kansas City in the early 1970s. But, if we wanted to go to a movie, we saved up pop bottles and cashed them in for a few dollars in refunds to buy tickets.

Such penny-pinching probably seems almost mythic to younger readers today—even in the midst of what's being called the "Great Recession." Doesn't everyone have the right to a cell phone, MP3 player, and text messaging? Thriftiness was part of daily life when Sharon and I were in our twenties, saving money to buy a business. Yes, we both had jobs, but we were putting away as much of our salaries as we could. We didn't send out for pizza. We didn't lease a fancy new car. We certainly didn't have a big-screen color TV.

Thrift is one of our basic values, and if you don't know and understand your values, your choices are liable to be haphazard and contradictory. Values are simply the decisive, underlying principles that knit a philosophical thread through your life.

Prudence is a basic value for me; being open to love and support is a value. Intellectual curiosity is a strong value of mine; that's why I embarked on the journey of discovery by which we transformed The Neenan Company from a struggling Butler franchise builder to an innovative business; and that eventually led me to teach "Business & You."

This whole book is based on my values. The stories are the flesh and the values are the bones. If we live conscious, active, learning-based lives, values help determine virtually every choice we make. Identifying them gives coherent shape to our personality, and makes honoring them more of an everyday occurrence.

It's a worthwhile exercise to reflect on the genesis of your values—take some time and tell yourself, or your loved ones, the stories that describe the provenance of what you believe in. It's important to refresh them, explain them, understand them, and act on them. Values are meaningless until they are used.

Do sea squirts have values? Certainly—security, for one, which they express when they send out their holdfast and stay put.

My values are an eclectic set of principles of which I have grown conscious over the years; aside from what's elsewhere in this book, several vitally important ones are below. They seem to be intrinsic to me and have grown outward from my heart to my hands.

Thrift

Sharon is incredibly prudent. We both value thrift, yet she much more than I. When we were a young married couple, saving all my earnings to buy a business, she sewed most of our clothes. For the better part of four years, we lived only on Sharon's $6,000 salary as a teacher, and that enabled us to build the nest egg with which we moved to Colorado and started in business. No, it wasn't arduous—being thrifty can be fun.

I drive an Audi sedan that's eleven years old. We've lived in the same house for thirty years now. It's the house in which we raised our four daughters; we recently remodeled it. Our second home, near San Diego, is a wonderful vacation getaway—and a fabulous investment that has appreciated more than 200 percent. It's comfy, but not excessive—3200 square feet. No pool.

I do have a lot of shirts—silk shirts, linen ones, cotton. Remember that jibe my long-ago girlfriend made about my shirts when I was young? My shirts are far less expensive than psychotherapy or a Porsche.

Trust

I believe in prudence. But I also practice trust, and the second is more important to me. I think it's one of the things I learned in Officer Candidate School long ago in the Army: Trust is a belief in yourself that you project to others. On the whole, I would rather be naïve than prudent.

The rewards are huge for me. For many years, one of my key colleagues, Randy Myers, has had permanent power of attorney for myself and for the Neenan Family Partnership. In the course of more than fifty investment undertakings, I've never pored over a spreadsheet; if Randy says it works, I believe it. He can and does sign checks and contracts for us. I can change them, but I never have.

He values the trust, and so do I.

Closely allied with trust is another characteristic: generosity. I am blessed with time, energy, and wealth, and I use these as currency to support other people's journeys whenever I can.

Persistence

Winston Churchill was asked to give a speech at the famous British boy's school, Harrow, in 1941, just about the time the tides of war began to turn in Britain's favor after four dark years. The headmaster urged the boys to pay the utmost attention to this great man. He'd been prime minister—twice. He'd won and lost more political battles than a dozen other men. Surely, the boys were about to hear something historic.

And they did. Churchill stood up, took his place at the lectern, and intoned a series of words that have entered into myth:

"Never give in. Never give in. Never, never, never, never—in nothing, great or small, large or petty—never give in, except to convictions of honor and good sense."

The legend is, that's all he said. That's not true (the famous quote comes in the middle of an address that took about ten minutes), but Churchill put his finger on one of the greatest of human virtues. Since he was uniquely qualified to say what he did, the quote, the story, and the idea have passed into myth.

Persistence is one of my strongest values, one I have exercised countless times in my own life. I simply don't quit. I have the ability to see that "no" is a rejection of my request, not of me. Luckily, I live in a time and place where almost everyone is given the opportunity for another chance.

Persistence brought me the fifty-dollar prize for newspaper subscriptions that I used to buy my own first pair of shoes. Finding passage across the Pacific on my way to Australia is another example—I headed to the West Coast, determined that I would find a job on a freighter and work my way across. I started in Long Beach, boarding ships, asking to see the purser, and asking for an interview with the captain. Ship after ship after ship, I was able to see the purser, but not the captain. I tried all the commercial ships in Long Beach, then Los Angeles, then made my way to Oakland, where—after soliciting almost one hundred ships—the captain of a Japanese freighter agreed to meet with me and hear my request.

"It's a great idea," he told me, "but you're one hundred years too late." He explained that jobs on ships were now in the hands of unions, and there was little or no direct traffic between the United States and Australia. Then he offered a suggestion: Go to the airport, use my student ID from the University of Missouri, and fly to Hawaii on the red-eye for seventy-five dollars. In Hawaii, I could get a job and buy passage to Australia.

"I know you are a hard worker because you visited all these ships, and I can see the determination in your eyes," the freighter captain told me. "Get over to Hawaii and carry some bricks for a while, and you can pay your passage to Australia in no time."

That night I was on the plane to Honolulu, following advice I would never have received had I not been persistent enough to visit all those ships. Precession, yes? When I got to Hawaii, I took a job carrying bricks at construction sites. I worked so hard, I wore out my gloves, and my hands bled—but I persevered, and after a few days the foreman declared me his bro and gave me a raise and the opportunity to work as much as I wanted.

You could say this looks like the result of chance: Sheer luck brought me to that Japanese freighter captain. No, it wasn't luck. As B.C. Forbes put it, "Diamonds are only lumps of coal that stuck to their jobs." People are not carbon atoms—we have the ability to choose.

One of my other values, passion, is a heck of an aid to persistence. I deeply wanted to get to Australia. I was *excited* to carry bricks to make money to get me there. I did so for three months. I wouldn't trade that experience for anything. In a very real sense, the calluses I got have stayed with me ever since.

Humor

Whatever you're doing, you ought to have fun doing it. There are many sorts of fun, not all humorous—it isn't "funny" when I'm out on a fifty-mile ride on my bike—but humor is a key part of a life in which fun is a significant part. Humor is one of the chief virtues Sharon adds to my life.

She must have gotten it from her father. Garwood Arthur Wells was one of those imposing, crusty guys who'd look straight at you and make you feel like you were experiencing radar.

When I went to ask him about marrying Sharon (yes, I really did that), I was more than a little bit nervous. He was a good father who treated his daughter well—in fact, just a few months before my proposal, he had given Sharon a car for a college graduation present. It was a brand new, shiny, black 1969 Dodge Charger, one of the famous "muscle cars" movie directors liked to use in chase scenes. When I asked "Gar" if I could marry his daughter, he didn't even take his eyes off the TV football game.

"Okay, you can have her, but the car stays."

"It's Sharon I want, not the car," I protested.

Then he took a moment to turn and face me. "David, I was kidding."

I used the same approach one day when I had lunch with the fellow from whom I bought my business. Reid Burton was an old-fashioned construction guy, and I had bought Burton Builders—but everyone told me a construction company needed to have the name of the owner on it, so customers would understand that you were putting your name and your reputation on the line. When the Casper troubles hit, I got a letter from Reid urging me to change the name.

So I invited him to lunch and told him I was indeed going to institute a name change.

"So, I guess this is the end of Burton Builders," he said.

"No, I'm changing my name to David Burton," I told him. It took him a minute to get it, but then he smiled.

Sometimes the joke's on me. Once upon a time in the late eighties, when I was trying to encourage all the Neenan Company managers to keep their doors open to their employees, I became annoyed with the continued proliferation of closed-door meetings in private offices. So, I ordered our maintenance supervisor one night to remove all the office doors in the building. The whole company was stunned the next day.

Next day after that, I went into my bathroom about 9:00 in the morning to use the toilet, and, as I was standing there, I heard my secretary gasp. I looked up and there she was—outside the open doorway. During the night the door to my bathroom had been removed. After a second, I started to laugh. There still aren't doors on offices in The Neenan Company, but I did manage to restore the door to my bathroom.

Forgiveness

In 1980, after I'd managed to extricate The Neenan Company and myself from the problems in Casper, I was driving one day along the freeway and felt I saw my dad on a peak in the Rockies. I realized then that he had provided the impetus for my life: He quit on his dream. I had witnessed the agonizing result, and resolved to pursue my dreams indomitably.

I wanted to communicate that to him, so I wrote a letter to him, flew back to Missouri, and visited his grave. I read the letter to my dad on October 10, 1980. "My life has turned into the greatest miracle," I told him, and described what I'd accomplished and what I wanted to further achieve. "The desire that burns white hot within me to see this purpose fulfilled comes from you, Dad. A day does not pass without me realizing that there's one giant slice of Jack Neenan in me. In many ways, I'm probably the most fortunate man alive, and I know it."

A literal view of reality would say I was just communicating with myself. I had been angry at my dad for twenty-one years because he drank too much, and he had made an awful decision to let Peter drive the car that fatal night in Reno. Two decades later, I wanted to come to peace with him, and I did. For almost two weeks I felt waves of joy.

The episode illustrates perfectly the meaning, and reward, of forgiveness. You often hear that forgiving is for the forgiver, and I find that exactly right. My anger at my dad was hampering my serenity, not his (I presume). The famous Alcoholics Anonymous steps in which recovering addicts make amends to those they have wronged—these are not designed just for the benefit of the victims of the drunk's bad behavior. They help lift the scourges of regret, fear, and bitterness on both sides.

The dictionary defines *forgiveness* this way: "To give up resentment or claim to requital." Notice the last part particularly— it says we let go of expectations of emotional recompense.

"If you are going to live a good life," a Croatian guide once told my coauthor Eric, "you must walk along with your neighbors. If you keep hold to the hate, you cannot even live with yourself." This from a woman whose neighbors, the Serbians, had decimated her country just fifteen years beforehand, leaving behind land mines that occasionally maim Croatian children to this day.

Vision

The realization that dawned on me in the Australian desert was not only that I was in the wrong place, doing the wrong thing, but that I had a purpose in life: *To be to my family as my uncle Jimmy had been to his* when he offered my mother financial assistance.

I knew I needed to achieve wealth to ensure that.

I knew I wanted to marry Sharon and start a family.

I had no idea that I would wind up buying a commercial construction company in a small Colorado city; raise four daughters; run into business trouble twice and meet the challenge; learn a great deal about business theory, personal growth, and helping humanity improve; and pass what I've learned on to thousands of people in hundreds of workshops around the world.

I couldn't have known. I simply set myself an objective and began to pursue it. I adopted a vision and set goals. If you were to consider vision a picture, goals are the pixels. Please, think expansively. Paint a big picture.

Most of those goals emerged as I went along, and became more specific along the way. My goal of achieving wealth evolved into one of owning a business, which evolved into buying a business, and then into buying a construction business. The more specific the goal, the more focused and effective the energy you can apply to it.

"I want to be famous." Great. How? "Um, I'll sing." Sing what? "Gospel music." Fine. Where and when? The answer: In her father's church down the street—which is how Aretha Franklin started her career. When she started, she couldn't have known that she would become an international music superstar.

There's a lot of blather about vision these days. Major corporations hire high-priced facilitators to conduct "visioning" exercises in which they paint their future. A vision should derive from your values. If you will permit me to continue the picture metaphor, values are how you frame your vision. I suppose a sea squirt's vision is to keep that holdfast cemented in place as long as it lives.

Please imagine a broader, more challenging, and worthwhile vision for yourself. The purpose of a vision, and the goals you adopt to achieve it, is to set yourself in motion, and then pay attention to the precessional effects. Keep setting goals and working toward them, and you will assuredly achieve something. Set your vision as high as you like, and then make your goals realistic challenges. Want to increase your wealth? Great. Adopt a goal of improving your net worth 10 percent this year.

A life without vision is pale. I believe there is hope in every human heart, and vision is simply that hope, given shape and set free.

Chapter 17

Abundance: An attitude that shapes your reality

We are all of us richer than we think we are. —Montaigne

It is the mind that makes the body rich. —Andrew Carnegie

Poised near a new multi-modal transit facility in my home city in Colorado is a large block of white marble that an African sculptor shaped into a graceful depiction of a human figure freeing himself from the bonds of everyday existence. It's a distinctive work, towering over passersby, expressive, a bit surrealistic. Until recently it was at the entrance to Old Town Fort Collins, and not at all like the more traditional pieces of Western art elsewhere in this small downtown historic district. A nearby bronze piece shows a cowboy looking down at the world, rope in hand, ready to tie up cattle. Its sixteen-ton, white marble counterpart, *Transcend,* suggested to viewers that all people can overcome whatever holds them down.

The statue cost a total of $100,000. It was paid for, and given to the people of Fort Collins, by well-off, local benefactors—the Neenan family trust.

Why would we do that? Shouldn't we keep our money in the bank, especially when one ought to be ever-ready for economic turmoil such as that which engulfed the world in late 2008? And what possessed me to hire an itinerant Zimbabwean artist to come to a white-bread, High Plains city and create an exotic piece of public art?

First of all, it was fun. I considered it an experiment in creating art, and it was. For four months Collen Nyanhongo toiled in the Colorado sunshine, a black man in a white city carving a piece of white marble to represent an abstract idea. "David," Collen told me later, "I appreciate the work. I appreciate the challenge. I really appreciate the new girlfriends!" So Collen had fun, too, and apparently a number of Fort Collins residents had fun with him.

Furthermore, it challenged the city. Not everyone liked it. Why not bring in another piece of mainstream art, something celebrating Colorado pioneers, or maybe even the Cheyenne people who inhabited this country before us? *Transcend* is ethereal, suggestive, highly personal. I heard a lot of guff about it.

I believe art is one of the two most expressive forms of human endeavor (music is the other). And, though some public art goes a bit far in pricking the sensitivities of the communities that give it space, the traditional statue in an urban plaza is often pointless pablum. I didn't want to sponsor that.

The whole adventure was catalyzed years ago in Las Vegas (not really my kind of place, but there I was) when I visited Steve Wynn's art gallery at the Bellagio. Here was $500 million in art, on display for anyone to look at, and one piece in particular captured my attention—a portrait of Picasso's mistress that he painted during World War II. It depicts two distinct sides of the woman's personality, and it provoked me to learn more about the painting so I could understand it. Thus, I learned more about Picasso and about World War II, both fascinating topics.

Why would Steve Wynn, a multimillionaire many times over, buy a priceless work of art, a painting that would be the pinnacle of his personal interior décor, and put it on public display?

Well, why would Bill Gates, one of the richest men on earth, turn over his self-made $35 billion fortune to a charitable foundation in an attempt to erase childhood illness around the world? Why would Warren Buffett do the same? Why did Andrew Carnegie, long before them, turn over his entire fortune— greatest in the world at the end of the nineteenth century—to philanthropic work?

Carnegie built thousands of libraries across North America, Great Britain, and other English-speaking lands. Many Carnegie libraries are still landmark public facilities in their home towns. They are the physical legacy of his fortune (see Chapter 20 for more about legacies). But the decision to distribute his fortune as he did is a reflection of an idea that is an even stronger legacy. Human beings tend to either hoard or share. I believe each choice is rooted in a personal paradigm: We believe in either scarcity or abundance. If we subscribe to scarcity, we keep our resources to ourselves, under the floorboards, metaphorically speaking. If we subscribe to abundance, we distribute our resources far and wide, especially to our families, friends, neighbors, and communities.

These two concepts, scarcity and abundance, form one of life's many yin-yang dualities. Each illuminates the other.

Scarcity says: There isn't enough. I have to protect and hoard what I have.

Abundance says: There's plenty. The more we share, the more we'll all have.

Both views of the world are true, if by *true* you mean an assertion for which you can muster facts and figures in support. But both are paradigms that determine not only how you view the underlying idea, but how you approach life. If you believe in scarcity, you believe in a win/lose world and are in cynical defense mode the moment you wake up. If you believe in abundance, each day holds promise.

Abundance is an attitude; so is scarcity. Either one can apply to money, food, love, energy, time, land, joy, hope, opportunity, chocolate—whatever.

We all know people whose frame of reference is obviously based in one philosophy or the other. If you're hooked on scarcity, fear of loss tends to make you grasping, aggressive, suspicious, and selfish.

If you believe in abundance, you're more generous, trusting, supportive, and optimistic. Those are the attitudes Paul Newman, one of my heroes, applied to life, enjoying great professional success, personal prosperity, a lot of fun (his hobby was grand prix racing!), a lifelong marriage—and creating a fabulously successful, nonprofit enterprise. Newman's Own, and the Newman's Own Foundation, have raised and donated more than $250 million to charities around the world. That's a quarter-*billion* bucks. Compare that to the average actor's legacy.

Belief in scarcity can reach equally large proportions. It likely hit its pinnacle with British philosopher Thomas Malthus' 1798 prediction that humankind's population would eventually exceed our subsistence ability, and starvation would overtake the human race. He projected population growth against food supplies and, presto, found that famine was inevitable. We'd all starve. That's scarcity! But he failed to foresee the astounding growth in agricultural productivity that has far outpaced population growth; today, there is not only enough food, there's more than enough, and developed societies such as ours are wallowing in obesity.

Recent revivals of Malthusian alarm (scarcity is popular!) continue to overlook the fact that human fertility rates are declining sharply as standards of living rise. Yes, there are still famines in various locales around the world, but the problem isn't the food supply, it's efficient distribution and equitable use of it. The same goes for energy; as Bucky Fuller pointed out, were we to interconnect the electrical grids of the Eastern and Western Hemispheres, we'd have more than enough power. Recent campaigns to create a "smart grid" reflect the fact that, by some estimates, up to a third of all power we produce is wasted by inefficiency.

Bucky spent a lot of time and energy illustrating the foolishness of the scarcity syndrome and the inherent potential for abundance. In the sixties, for instance, he figured out that there was enough room in New York City for half the human race to wander about on the streets, and for the other half to lie down and sleep inside. Human population has grown since then, so today it might require adding in Long Island. That's not a land shortage.

Notice, too, that those who believe in scarcity tend to paint their positions as not just true, but The Truth, demanding obedience. Scarcity salesmen favor impending events—sign up *now* or the opportunity will be gone forever. Wow. Gone forever is the ultimate in scarcity, isn't it? Union workers who will shut down a company for "job security" are hooked on scarcity—this job, at this company, or else, forever. There's no other work at all for them to do?

Believing in abundance does not mean abandoning prudence. Yes, this is another lovely paradox—one of my favorites, because it reminds me that while the universe's potential is infinite, it is not guaranteed. An investment adviser who says astounding wealth will come your way if you sink all your savings into gold (this happened to my co-author's wife) is operating from greed, not abundance. I would not devote all my resources to investing in gold; nor would I use all my wealth to support public art.

Nor does sharing my own abundance, and proselytizing my belief in it, mean I must retire to a monastery and live on bread and water. Andrew Carnegie did not abandon his homes (one was a Scottish estate) to go live in a shack while he spent twenty years building more than three thousand libraries, founding the Carnegie Institute of Technology, creating Carnegie Hall in New York, building the Palace of Peace in the Hague. Sharon and I have more than one home, and have been grateful for our opportunity to travel the world, spend lots of time with friends and family, and provide ourselves life-rewards such as an annual trip to the Seychelles.

Asked to describe the moment most representing abundance in my life, I'd recall a family vacation Sharon and I and our four daughters took years ago when our youngest, Lexi, was old enough to travel far. We flew to Hong Kong, then on to Thailand. We all rode elephants (they don't go very fast); we watched a cobra show; a monkey at a street carnival grabbed Lindsay's earring and ate it; and a "snake" (actually a rope) landed in Sharon's lap. We all still laugh about that. And I remember, too, the moment Sharon and I felt our future as potential parents was most bleak. She had just miscarried a few months before and declared, "I don't think I'll ever have a baby!" But she was already pregnant again, and Jessica was born seven months later.

That trip to Asia with all four of our daughters wasn't cheap, and it illustrates the true nature of financial abundance. As I've said before, money is just a convenient measuring device that is also a most practical tool. It's what I paid Collen with, what I used to buy that sixteen-ton block of marble, how I hired the truck that brought the rock to Fort Collins from Marble, Colorado. I'm passing my financial abundance on to my four daughters, but in a measured way: They each receive income from a trust, as long as they are pursuing an education or working for the benefit of society. Today, two are teachers, one is helping the indigenous people of Alaska, and one works in a hospital in Denver.

And simply believing in abundance does not make it so—it does not fall from the sky. Work, vision, commitment, and integrity are the keys to furthering abundance. Commit to a purpose that's larger than yourself, and you are on the road to abundance.

Abundance also does not support abuse. If energy and land are sufficient for human needs, that's no cause to squander either—just the opposite, in fact. If you're still driving around in a gas-guzzler that gets five miles per gallon, that's waste, not abundance. A sixty-room, 100,000-square-foot mansion? A $50,000 watch? Please.

Art has come to mean so much to me that Sharon and I created our own foundation, Tessa ("Asset" backward) to promote art appreciation and education. It attracted the interest of two friends who had long been gallery owners in California and Colorado, Larry Hartford and Torleif Tanstad. On retirement, they donated to Tessa the bulk of their $3 million inventory, and now Tessa has one of the finest art libraries in Colorado, and a collection of paintings with which we can mount several great shows. Our support of Collen's sculpting work in Old Town Fort Collins prompted the local development authority to schedule a public-art-creation each summer; Collen's statue has been moved and a new artist will set up shop there every year, though probably not with a $100,000 price tag.

Not that large sums are necessarily what mark a distinctive work of art. I've an incredibly meaningful painting I acquired in Vietnam for one hundred dollars that depicts a wartime amputee on crutches, happily teaching math to young students. The glyphs on the picture say, "Life is good even to an invalid after the war."

See how abundance works? As Goethe said, once you become fully committed to an endeavor, then the means come your way to accomplish it.

We are either prisoners—or the greatest beneficiaries—of our own attitudes. It's our choice.

Bucky called abundance our human birthright. And remember what he called truth—diminishing error. Every time we take action based on a belief in abundance, I believe we are incrementally moving humanity closer to the truth of abundance. There is more than enough for us all. As E.E. Cummings put it, *"I thank you God for this most amazing day; for the leaping greenly spirit of trees and a blue true dream of sky; and for everything which is natural which is infinite which is yes."*

Chapter 18

Excuses: The "reasons" we duck responsibility

Freedom is what you do with what's been done to you.
—Jean-Paul Sartre

Taking responsibility every moment of every day is a tall order: Being responsible for our every word; our choices, big and small; our moods; our intentions; our very being? Making conscious decisions based on our values? Turning all those decisions into effective action? We all fall short, including me. This can be conscious or not; benign or malicious; willful or unintentional. However it occurs, the most prominent symptom, if one regards evading responsibility as an ailment, is almost always an excuse.

There is an abundance of these: *I didn't know. What choice did I have? It's Joe's fault. She started it. Everybody else does it.*

I'd like to tell you I have left excuses behind, but an accurate report would be, instead, that I strive to do so as much as possible. Let's say I am successful most often when I am conscious of my actions, but less so when I am unaware and need the sort of hero

Bucky Fuller referred to—someone who points out to me the invisibility of a mistake I'm making, such as my physician friend who observed my toxic mood.

And my "reasons" for embracing that toxic mood I was in? I couldn't help it. Disaster loomed. It wasn't fair. It certainly wasn't my fault.

Excuses all. Until my physician acquaintance helped me see reality, I'd have defended those excuses with every morsel of self-justification I had. When we are afraid, we cling fiercely to what our subconscious brainstem wrongly tells us is our only life raft. Blame it on someone else; cry to the skies for justice; declare the threat so great that we must act such and such—all these are approaches that render us victims. Excuses enable avoidance of responsibility; they prevent taking corrective action and attempt to enlist our family, friends, and community in our evasion.

Most importantly, excuses evade reality. No matter what we say or think or fear, the fact is that we make our own paths in life. We decide how to face every day, every person, every event.

My coauthor Eric bluntly puts it this way: "Your fate is your choice." People object ferociously to that idea. What if you're hit by a car? Get polio? Are laid off from your job? Those sorts of things do happen. But what happens next is still your choice, harsh as it may seem. As I have so often learned, taking responsibility is the only path to growth or peace or health or whatever I wish from life—and specifically what I wish from the challenge facing me.

No better example exists for this stringent notion than that of Viktor Frankl. Seized by Nazi troops from a peaceable existence as a psychiatrist in Vienna, he was sent to four concentration camps, eventually winding up at Auschwitz. He survived the twentieth century's greatest evil by concluding that, no matter how dire the circumstances, only he could, or would, take responsibility for his life.

What could be more dire than to be imprisoned at Auschwitz? Nonetheless, Frankl chose to use his medical and psychiatric skills to help his fellow prisoners survive as best they could—and face extermination with dignity when it came to that, as it did for more than one million at Auschwitz-Birkenau. When disease swept the camp even as liberation neared, he reminded his fellows that, believe it or not, things could be worse. In his astounding book, *Man's Search for Meaning* (which appears first in the list of suggested reading at the end of this book), Frankl writes, "I said that even in this Europe in the sixth winter of the Second World War, our situation was not the most terrible we could think of. Whoever was still alive had reason for hope."

Talk about not making excuses! If a prisoner at Auschwitz can forego surrendering to despair, then who among us can claim there is no choice?

The World War II experience led Jean-Paul Sartre to fashion his philosophy, which says that we are all in charge of our destinies. In fact, that is what gives our lives significance.

"It is only in our decisions that we are important," Sartre declares. "We are alone, with no excuses. That is the idea I shall try to convey when I say that man is condemned to be free. Condemned, because he did not create himself, yet, in other respects is free; because, once thrown into the world, he is responsible for everything he does."

Sartre identified the excuses people use to justify evading responsibility. I have modified and adapted them to these six:

- Helplessness: "What can I do about it?" This was one excuse offered by millions of Germans and other Europeans who stood by while the Nazis seized the continent and murdered six million people in concentration camps.

- Innocence: "I didn't start this." This is why Serbs and Croats, Israelis and Palestinians, or Hindus and Muslims have been killing each other for generations.

- Herd behavior: "Everyone else is doing it." This is why teenagers drink, smoke, and have sex; peer pressure leaves them feeling they have little choice.

- Survival: "I'm just looking out for myself." It's why inside traders and commodities manipulators cheat investors.

- Higher authority: "God told me to." Billions of people through the ages have claimed this excuse, from Catholic priests who put people on the rack, to Muslim terrorists who bomb innocents, to fundamentalist Mormons who say God commands that fourteen-year-old girls endure sexual abuse by elderly men. They are only trying to evade responsibility for choices they make. The soldiers who perpetrated the My Lai massacre—they were just following orders. SS guards? Orders.

- Appeal to emotions: "I couldn't help it, I was afraid." So said the lawsuit of a Florida worker who alleged a phobia of black people for a disability claim. And the courts backed her up!

Of course there are many more excuses, most of which are variations or embellishments of these six: "I already know the answer," say those unwilling to receive new information. "I don't want to," say people assigned a difficult task.

You hear a lot these days about accountability, but the word has been bastardized by euphemistic excess into meaninglessness. It seems to have morphed into "Yes, I did it—but I have an excuse." Remember when the governor of New York, former take-no-prisoners state attorney-general Eliot Spitzer, was exposed as a frequent customer of high-priced callgirls, sometimes using campaign funds to book hotel rooms? When he faced reality and resigned, he declared that he was "taking responsibility," yet he did little to demonstrate this responsibility aside from giving up a job he was going to lose anyway. With his hapless wife standing by his side, he blamed "personal failings," but neglected to describe what he would do to change them (for example, get help for an obvious sex addiction) or to make amends to his family.

It's been interesting to watch Tiger Woods face the same sort of issue. Notice how public sentiment about Tiger has softened a bit as he seems to be taking action to address another obvious sex addiction? That's what happens when you take responsibility: People rally round you. Excuses keep people victims. Taking responsibility is what makes heroes. I don't want to call Woods any sort of hero—years will pass before it becomes clear whether he has, indeed, taken responsibility. But at least he didn't blame his troubles on anyone else, on or off the golf course.

Excuses are endemic in modern life. Addicts say that, whether it is heroin, whiskey, or Hostess Twinkies they put in their mouths, they can't help it—they're addicted. Sure, they are. But addiction means that they cannot stop once they start; it does not mean that they must have that drink to begin with. It is a choice for which they are only making excuses—helplessness, in this case.

You can even watch people make excuses for others. Witness the mother who bails her son out of jail after his fourth drunk-driving arrest: "Robby's just a high-spirited young man." How about the wife who sticks up for a husband who hasn't worked for years: "There aren't any jobs at his level these days."

Are excuses invariably wrong? This is the crux of the existential dilemma: If we are irrevocably responsible for our fates, how stringently do we impose this responsibility? When a battered wife is too afraid to leave her husband—even after he's broken her arm twice—and declines to press charges, is that just Excuse Number Six? Myriad are the women who have pressed charges, received restraining orders, tried to escape, and been gunned down for their trouble. No wonder they're afraid! But Sartre's unflinching view of life—as well as the battle-hardened view of domestic violence workers—holds that reality offers no options aside from taking responsibility. In this case, a battered woman must do what she can to achieve safety and separation. Seeking help would be a great first step. Staying put improves nothing.

As it happens, fear is the most difficult excuse to identify. Aren't there times when fear is wholly justified, when it should guide our choices? Sure. If you're stuck on the edge of a cliff and jumping off would be fatal, then the universe is sending you important information in the form of your fear. It's when fear is used as the reason for inaction, or inappropriate reaction, that it's the most troublesome excuse. My fear about that $58 million lawsuit was not irrational, and I took some appropriate action— hiring a great lawyer to defend The Neenan Company. My bitter, resentful mood was inappropriate reaction, and that's what I had to change once I recognized it.

I'm grateful that my life has presented none of the most appalling conditions under which fear rears its head. If you were an ordinary citizen in Holland during the Nazi occupation, you had good reason to be afraid of helping Jews hide. You might well be sent to a death camp, too, if discovered. That excuse didn't stop the Dutch citizens who helped harbor Anne Frank, her sister, and parents in their house for four years.

I've undoubtedly used all six excuses in my life and have been tempted by many more. How come it took me so long to quit smoking? *I was helpless;* nicotine addiction is incredibly powerful. What about when I went along with my high school buddies in delinquent behavior? *Everyone does that.*

I am proudest of the moments when I set aside excuses, though it wasn't pride that I was aiming for. Remember when people advised me to sue or file bankruptcy to escape the Casper mess? *That's what everyone does,* I was told. *It's a matter of survival. Listen to your fears; you should be afraid. You didn't start this problem; there is no other choice; you're helpless.* It was a heck of a crisis: Five of the six possible excuses came into play.

No one lives an excuse-free life. Yes, saying so calls to mind Excuse Number Three (herd behavior), but the point I am trying to make is that an excuse is symptomatic of a mistake. It's claiming victimhood. Self-punishment accomplishes nothing. My goal is to recognize such moments, identify the excuse, and make a rational, responsible decision about what to do.

Excuses weaken our taste of the banquet of life. I believe the more I recognize and set aside excuses, the more I will be alive, fulfilled, useful, and loved.

Chapter 19

Sustainability: Waste is the problem

The ultimate intention behind sustainable entrepreneurship is to add value. The question is, how does one define value?
—Lindsay Neenan

There I was, in The Neenan Company's east side men's bathroom, cleaning out the urinal. It's an especially unsavory chore, as this is a no-flush appliance that uses a filter to screen out uric acid and other chemicals before releasing the waste into the sewer. It works well; but, every month, the filter must be replaced, which involves reaching into the device, loosening the filter with a special tool, and pulling it out. The smell is brutally foul. I find myself looking for my old Army gas mask.

I'm the chairman of the company. Why am I doing this?

It's so unpleasant, hardly anyone else will. And the problem perfectly illustrates my perspective on one of the hot topics of today, sustainability.

The Neenan Company is committed to resource conservation, and this urinal saves fifty thousand gallons of water a year, about half the average household's use, just in one appliance. Water's a precious resource in Colorado; saving fifty thousand gallons is great, but using a device that requires maintenance so unpleasant almost no one will do it—not so great.

We also have a low-flush urinal (one pint) in our other men's bathroom. There's no filter, so it does use a little water—about one-eighth that of a standard urinal. In other words, this one saves more than forty-three thousand gallons of water a year. It does require a standard house-cleaning wipe-down periodically.

Which urinal is the better choice?

Answering questions like that is one of the reasons The Neenan Company has adopted numerous sustainability measures: vegetation on part of our roof, sun sensors that turn off the lights on the appropriate side of our building when there's adequate sunlight, skylights to provide light in our workshop center, hiring a landscaping company that minimizes use of power tools. Our building has received platinum certification from an organization called ClimateWise Colorado.

Our employee green team astounded (and alarmed) everyone a while back when they surreptitiously removed all the personal wastebaskets in the office. The idea was to reduce overall waste. Milder strategies hadn't worked, so one day one hundred employees showed up to discover their trash cans gone. The event was called, "Dude, where's my trash can?"

At first the reaction was not happy. You can figure out for yourself the excuses people apply to not recycling. Trash was dumped on green team members' desks; complaints were rampant. But attitudes slowly shifted. Field superintendents called for advice on how they could curtail waste. Today the Neenan office has diverted 83 percent of our previous waste by recycling, composting, and other strategies. One building project reduced construction waste by 88 percent.

All this is well and good; it has not only saved resources, it has saved us money and helped us to provide expert answers when clients ask about sustainable initiatives in their building designs. Believe me, they do ask—it's one of the most common criteria we deal with in the building industry these days. And it's spreading throughout the business world; my daughter Lindsay calls it an "avalanche," and made sustainability the topic of her master's thesis.

But I think the sustainability phenomenon has so far overlooked some fundamentals of effective progress. Installing devices such as waterless urinals is applying small technical answers to a much bigger problem that is largely adaptive.

Sustainable is a perfectly useful term that has lately become a catch-phrase up for grabs by anyone seeking the cachet it confers. We've got sustainable tourism, sustainable agriculture, sustainable business, sustainable this and that, even sustainable underwear.

But what is *sustainable?*

To me, it describes an activity that can be beneficially maintained for a long period of time. Unsustainable describes an activity that depletes its base, so it will eventually run out.

In my home state of Colorado, for instance, water resource managers talk about "consumptive" uses for water, where the resource is used irreplaceably, and where, if the entire supply is used this way, there would be no more. Luckily, nature resupplies water; but there isn't an infinite store of it at any given time. Some of the rivers near my home in Fort Collins run dry at some points in late summer; all the water has been withdrawn for irrigation and urban use, consumptive uses that leave nothing in the river for others, including fish.

Obviously, that wouldn't be sustainable over time—were it not for the snow that piles up each winter in the Rockies and replenishes the water each spring.

One can debate the wisdom of our reliance on scarce water; innumerable arguments have taken place on that exact topic for centuries, and it is certainly worthwhile to examine whether a use for something is wise and productive in the long run.

These discussions are engaging, but they seem to compose virtually the entire sustainability debate today, which focuses almost exclusively on technical answers (precise and mechanical), rather than adaptive (system-changing). Such arguments overlook what I consider a key facet of the whole issue. Waste is the most common activity that's truly unsustainable; waste is pandemic in our society—in business, home, and government; and, by waste, I mean more than what goes in the trash can or down the drain. I mean waste in human interaction and enterprise.

In the construction industry, waste was reckoned by W. Edwards Deming at 42 percent. In my company, on one occasion, we measured it; the waste came in at 27 percent. The best performance Deming had found at any company was 21 percent waste—in other words, only 79 percent efficiency.

Mull that over for a minute. Waste—sheer, unadulterated, unproductive squandering of resources, whether they be paper or profits—ranges from one-fifth to almost half. And this is in business, which is supposed to be the profit-driven exemplar of efficiency!

Imagine all the paper, energy, water, and other environmental resources chewed up by that waste, not to mention the money. Where does the waste come from? I see two key problems:

- Lack of communication. The architect's plans call for an eight-foot ceiling; the new MRI machine for which the clinic is being built is 8' 6" high. Yikes! Plans are redrawn, framing has to be redone, new lumber ordered by special delivery. This is financially and environmentally wasteful.

That's not sustainable.

In construction, an exotic practice has arisen to cover such all-too-frequent occurrences. Change-orders are the rule of the day in building projects—sometimes necessary, more often not. The average in our industry is 12–20 percent.

- Lack of trust. The architect doesn't believe the estimator's numbers; the sales rep doesn't believe the interior designer's estimates. The client winds up footing the bill for extra structural steel and carpet upgrades.

Years ago, when I set about to change exactly this sort of problem at the Neenan Company, I hired an architect to join our staff. He was promptly kicked out of the American Institute of Architects for, I don't know, consorting with the enemy.

Things have improved a bit; we now have more than twenty architects on our staff, and many do belong to AIA. We also have engineers, interior designers, financial experts, planning and development experts, construction management professionals, and market research experts. We gather as many relevant disciplines for each project as are needed, put them all in the same room, and guide them toward a collaboration that saves waste. *That* saves time, materials, money, and energy. We come up with a project bid that we believe in, and we very rarely re-bid.

We seek to promote common-sense efficiency in most of our activities. If we're building a school in a small, rural town, and none of the town's three plumbers can handle all the work on the school, we'll put together a consortium of the three—much better than bringing in a larger plumbing firm from a city three hours away. When our multi-discipline project team needs to visit, they all fly in one morning, make sure they meet with the clients in the morning, the subcontractors at lunch, and the engineers in the afternoon. Then they head home.

That's what I believe is sustainable. To state it formally:

Waste elimination and value creation are the basis of sustainability and this can only be accomplished by people collaborating across disciplines in a mood of trust.

The Neenan Company green team exemplifies this. A half-dozen of our employees regularly meet to discuss what can be done to minimize waste, both physical and organizational. They collaborate. Yes, they all cooperated on "Dude, where's my trash can"—which got us a great deal of publicity in Fort Collins, and has spread to other organizations.

The damage caused by waste is hardly confined to the construction industry. The average illiteracy rate among America's school children is 30 percent. Almost a third of our kids cannot functionally read or write! What a waste of human potential. And how will we enlist those kids in energy conservation campaigns, say? "Please turn out the lights," stickers advise in more and more small public bathrooms and other such facilities. If a third of the people using them can't read, that's not very effective.

Construction projects that go seriously awry often wind up in court. Have you ever seen how much paper is consumed by legal action—not to mention our old friends time, money and energy?

Sustainability depends on diverse disciplines working together in an atmosphere of trust. The key question is not: How much value can you extract? It's: How much value can you convey?

I see sustainability consultants these days, offering advice on meeting LEED (Leadership in Energy and Environmental Design) standards, driving around in huge SUVs between client visits. Is that conveying value, or extracting it? One such "consultant" was hired by a client of ours; he reviewed their building design, informed them that it was quite good and he had very few suggestions—and sent them an invoice for ten thousand dollars! That's not sustainability, that's old-fashioned flim-flammery.

I wouldn't argue that we can change it all. But what if we just got rid of the 25 percent that lies between the most efficient operations and the most wasteful? The difference would be profound.

I probably won't live to see it, but I'll keep seeking it in my daily life. If we all did that, it would happen.

Chapter 20

Legacy: Spreading the opportunity

How wonderful it is that nobody need wait a single moment before starting to improve the world. —Anne Frank

I came to Russia with a pocket full of dollar bills. I spent them all on postcards I never used.

This was April, 1992, when Sharon and I made our first trip to Moscow to present "Business & You." I'd been told that a dollar bill was the magic key to traveling there, that dollars were a universal currency good for almost anything in the aftermath of communism's collapse. True enough, I found.

But what to buy? As we made the obligatory tour of Red Square, gawking at the Kremlin and St. Basil's Cathedral, I kept encountering young Russian kids selling postcards, 10 for $1. They were poor quality, with grainy, blurred photos from the 1950s of the Bolshoi Ballet, Lenin's tomb, other iconic Russian images. I'd pass along a buck and get a handful of crummy postcards in return, then toss them as soon as I could.

"David," Sharon asked, "what on earth are you doing?"

I thought about it. The answer was simple: Those kids were me. Forty years earlier, I'd been selling one-dollar subscriptions to the Columbia Missourian, hoping that they would be my ticket to a better life. I was recycling those dollars a lifetime later to other kids taking their first steps on the path of entrepreneurship.

Just as I had done as a boy, those youngsters at Red Square were answering one of the great economic issues of our time: How do you turn almost nothing into something?

That question holds the key to my legacy.

Though popular conception paints the term *legacy* as a monolithic, discrete thing, I don't think it's that simple. One can have many legacies, deriving from family, work, cause, and avocation. And any human being can build legacies; it's not limited to artists and politicians, entrepreneurs and visionaries. It can be as simple as planting a tree: Every autumn my coauthor helps press cider at his wife's family's heritage apple orchard, a century-old legacy left by her great-grandfather.

My business legacy is the Neenan Company, a soundly run enterprise that supplies useful work to more than two hundred employees and hundreds of vendors, and supports many families. I believe the spread of Archistruction™ through the design-build industry will bear my fingerprints on into the future, too.

The typical success path in business is to build a thriving enterprise, then sell it off or combine it with some other enterprise, retire, and play golf. I've resisted selling or merging The Neenan Company, because invariably either would extract value rather than carry it forward. Workers are laid off, budgets are cut. Many of the key figures at The Neenan Company have been my business companions for three decades. How could I sleep at night knowing liquidation of their jobs was my ultimate business legacy?

My personal legacy is as a father and husband—Sharon and I have been married forty-two years, something very few couples manage, even though millions fully intend a lifetime together at the start. We have raised four fine daughters, all of whom are young adults leading productive lives and contributing to the world around us. They will carry our lives and ideas (some of them, anyway) on into the future. That includes the idea that they can and should learn entirely new things about which I have no clue!

My personal legacy is also myself—at sixty-eight, I'm mostly healthy, fit, and long ago left behind the ugly habits of youth, such as cigarettes, that some people pursue to their deaths. I don't mean to tempt the gods here, but I do my best to treat my body and my spirit like the gifts they are. I also do my best to extend that same courtesy to my family, my friends, and my community.

"Business & You" is a legacy, also. How many thousands of people have learned something at workshops I've led, I can't say. I'm confident there are many, though.

Notwithstanding all that, as I passed sixty, I began to experience a longing to leave behind something larger still, although "larger" is an inexact word that unfortunately sounds as if size is what matters. What I was seeking was a way to cast a thread of change into human life that would reflect my values onto future generations. Theorists about human purpose sometimes talk of an "infinite game," a poorly-worded phrase that refers to something that's not a game at all. The purpose is not the creation of a specific outcome (such as to score more touchdowns, or even make more money) but the continued growth of the meaning of something—in other words, something that outlives you. Something sustainable.

For instance, a quarterback who throws the winning touchdown has won a finite game. Maybe the story of that touchdown has some currency later on, as might several of John Elway's touchdowns. A single, winning touchdown is a novelty that does not cast into the future a change in human life. The early pioneers who founded the National Football League, however, did. They set in motion a (so far) infinite game.

Okay, sports analogies are shallow. A better one would be Alcoholics Anonymous. Bill Wilson and Dr. Bob Smith, the cofounders of AA, created something in 1935 that has now reached millions of people and healed many millions of ruined lives, long after its originators passed on. Aldous Huxley called Wilson "the greatest social architect of the twentieth century." AA continues its spread around the world today, saving lives and repairing broken families every day.

I wanted to take part in something like that.

But I had no idea what it might be. Then, by chance one day in 2004, I was invited to hear a talk by a South American social activist at Colorado State University, the big college in my home city. I walked into the room in a cynical frame of mind; I left inspired. Hernando de Soto is a Swiss-educated Peruvian economist working to change what may be the single greatest impediment to economic opportunity worldwide. Hernando himself is a bespectacled, enthusiastic, highly-educated visionary who sometimes renders such arcane and complex information that the simple majesty of his message is hard to refine. I'm lucky I saw him in person, because I was immediately transfixed. Here was a guy who just wanted to offer the whole world the opportunity I'd had.

Briefly: Of the six billion people on the planet, five billion are not entitled to the economic opportunity most of us in the developed world enjoy. I use the word "entitled" because it conveys almost exactly the problem.

We have title to our homes, our businesses, our savings, our property—our identities. We have birth certificates, deeds, passports, addresses, Social Security numbers, marriage certificates, drivers licenses, bank accounts. I've had all those, and more. Stock certificates, loan agreements, tax returns, employment contracts, building contracts—they record the path of my life's numerous enterprises.

Five billion people do not have any of that—those boys selling postcards in Russia in 1992, for the most part, didn't. Most individuals live in unnamed, unnumbered places. No formal record has been made of their birth—their very existence! They have no official identity, no record of owning anything, no assets recognized by any government. What they do have, what calls to my soul, is ambition and desire, aspiration and hope. But they have no platform on which to sing their song, the melody Thoreau mentioned.

Think of it. Suppose you couldn't prove who you are, where you live, what you "own." Walk into a bank and see what happens, whether you want to leave money there or leave with money. Try to get a phone line. Suppose you want a job that lasts more than a day—see if you can get that.

If you don't even "exist," how can you grow and prosper?

Hernando recognized this problem in the 1980s and set out to see if it could be solved. Though the untitled people of the world lack documents and records that we take for granted, they do have houses, cattle, spinning looms, and other assets that are tangible but not fungible—to use the technical terms; their assets can't be exchanged or substituted in order to settle debt. If we help these folks record their lives and livelihoods in official terms, we can welcome them into the modern economy. That gives a platform to their dreams.

In Hernando's home country, he helped millions of Peruvians, living on the margins of society, become fully entitled citizens. Couples who had previously lacked a record of their marriage, for instance, now found themselves able to claim government benefits, get jobs, send their children to school, and buy homes. The economic impact was profound, not just for Peruvian society, but for enterprises within it. Telefonica, a communications company that enlisted Hernando's help, saw its market value rise from $52 million to more than $2 billion.

Hernando's organization, the Institute for Liberty and Democracy, now works around the world, helping more than fifty countries address the problem of their un-titled citizens, who are known as "extra-legals." His work has been embraced by the United Nations and USAID (United States Agency for International Development), which issued a call in 2007 for ILD principles to be adopted worldwide.

Of course, all this is soul music to me. So many of the facets of my life that bring it meaning derive from those simple advantages I enjoyed by right of birth in a developed society. I exist and can prove it. I have property and title to it. Sharon and I are married and have four fine daughters—and we can prove it.

Suppose I could help extend those simple foundations of modern life to billions?

Understand that the idea is not to "give" people anything other than what they are entitled to as a simple fact of existence. If we are to accept Sartre's dictum that we are condemned to be free as a fact of our birth, then the least we can do for most of humanity is to accord them the basic rights that come with that existence.

Hernando focuses on these five rights: personal property; rule of law; open banking; limited liability; and trial by jury. It's hard for those of us in developed countries to realize that so many people do not enjoy these rights we take for granted, but it's true.

Bucky was right—abundance is our birthright. To claim it, human beings need a solid step to stand on. If ever there was an existential dilemma, this is it: We have not extended to five billion people the basic modern-day rights of existence. We need to do that.

I believe the result will be an unimaginable harvest of individual enterprise, cultural growth, and widespread abundance.

Let me be clear. The idea is not to create five billion multimillionaires. Making money is part of it, but making money as its own end is not sustainable. I don't want to measure this effort just in dollars. ILD's goal is to create a platform for healthy, productive family lives around the world.

Supporting that has brought me a sense of meaning that adds immeasurably to my life. I've donated time and, yes, money to ILD. I've recruited dozens of new supporters to Hernando's cause, and I invite you to join us at www.ild.org.pe.

Recently, I made use of my own personal perspective to boost my support for ILD. Legitimizing people is of huge benefit to the businesses that operate in Third World countries; their revenues and assets grow as their constituent economies grow. Why not take part in that quintessentially capitalist result? With the help of two close friends, Bill Reynolds and Doug Schatz, we established Live

Capital LLC, a for-profit adjunct to ILD that will use business principles to further the effort. As Hernando's work around the globe uncovers startup investment opportunities, the LLC acts as a sort of venture capital firm, boosting enterprise development. A share of the gains will be turned over to ILD's nonprofit operations in a format resembling that used by Paul Newman's Newman's Own enterprises.

The details of this effort are vitally important to me; I believe in enterprise. More than nineteen thousand children starve to death every day, and it's not because there is insufficient food on earth; it's because so much of humanity is outside the developed economy we take for granted. Bringing them inside our tent makes the world better for us all.

But my real message is that no amount of personal achievement brings much meaning until you extend your own wealth to others—economic wealth, personal energy, spiritual wealth. Whatever you *have* is simply the bricks and mortar of your own life. What you send onward becomes a light beam that, each time it reaches someone else, is not consumed but magnified. That's not only sustainable; it's the ultimate in sustainability.

I want to shine on. I hope you do, too.

Chapter 21

Health: The best treatment is taking action

Measure your health by your sympathy with morning and Spring. —Thoreau

I couldn't get off my bike.

For dedicated long-distance bicycle riders such as me, that may not sound like any kind of problem. We welcome hours on our bikes, pedaling miles and miles up and down hills, across country, out and back along quiet secondary roads. Near my Colorado home there are dozens of farm roads skirting cornfields, beet fields and cow pastures by which I have pedaled hundreds of times. In San Diego, near my second home, I discovered that the best riding territory came through talking myself past the gate at Pendleton Marine Corps Base. At the time I encountered difficulty dismounting, I was riding more than 200 miles a week, racking up thousands of miles a year. It was July, 2009, and I had already covered 3,800 miles so far that year. I could hardly wait to get on the bike, five or more days a week. So… Can't get off the bike? What's the problem?

Big problem: Something had gone awry in my skeletal structure, and I was hurting so much, my joints were so painful, that I literally couldn't get off my bike after my usual 50-mile rides. The best time of day for me was when I went to bed. The worst—getting up. Some mornings I literally had to crawl at first. I couldn't shut the doors on my car. My morning stretching routine was agony. It started in spring of '09, and as it grew worse, for three months I had no quality of life. Zero.

Something was seriously wrong.

I've led a wonderfully healthy life and have had little need (except for the 1976 racquetball accident) to patronize the American health care system. I eat well, drink little, don't smoke, exercise regularly, stretch and strengthen every morning—and with all that, here I was, at 67, barely able to move. I'm too young for this, I told myself. I don't go to the doctor very much, but…

Let it be said that for me to complain at 67 that I'm too young for health trouble is fairly remarkable and reflects the change in human life wrought by modern medicine and lifestyle knowledge. When I was growing up people were largely considered old, infirm and used-up by the time they reached 60. "Hope I die before I grow old," sang the Who's Roger Daltrey in 1966. Yet Daltrey is still singing at the age of 66, and, as the saying goes, 60 is the new 40. "Isn't it a bit unnerving that doctors call what they do 'practice'," jested George Carlin; but the fact is, millions of people are living active, healthy lives at an age that people once considered old and decrepit. Some gerontologists believe there is no real reason human beings cannot live active, healthy lives well beyond 100.

And now I was at a point of despair when "old and decrepit" seemed a perfect description for me.

That's when I called on my lifelong experience with facing challenge, and made a decision to do whatever I could to alleviate the problem. I would try anything, go anywhere, talk to anyone.

First I visited a local rheumatologist. He tentatively diagnosed me with polymyalgia rheumatica, a chronic form of muscle pain that's similar to rheumatoid arthritis, though not as acute. I wasn't quite ready to accept that, so I booked myself into the Mayo Clinic in Scottsdale, Arizona, for a comprehensive diagnostic workup in September, 2009.

At the Mayo Clinic, "comprehensive" is an understatement.

A diagnostic visit here is like a trip to boot camp. Every day you are handed an itinerary of tests and consultations; every evening you visit a scheduler who draws up your itinerary for the next day. Each day you sit down with one or more physicians who explain what they are learning about you. Next day—more tests, more physicians, more results.

I gave blood multiple times a day, probably 50 vials in that week. That's a lot of blood. I was X-rayed, scanned, probed, stretched, scoped, analyzed, sampled, sized, palpated and poked.

I learned I didn't have lupus.

It wasn't rheumatoid arthritis.

Not Lyme disease.

I learned that my right hip will probably wear out in 10-15 years.

Finally, after five days of testing, I received three inches of paperwork, was told I did indeed have polymyalgia rheumatica, as well as sero-negative inflammatory disease, and was led directly to the pharmacy where they handed me a glass of water and two pills and said: "Take these now."

I did.

Relief started almost immediately, but that was the easy part. Remember that Asian saying, the easy road *is* the hard road? Our society is far too fond of the notion that medicine consists of going to a doctor, who declares: "You have X. Here, take Y. Your problems are over." Wrong.

You cannot plan to just take a pill and be healthy any more than you can plan to buy lottery tickets and be wealthy. I know this, so I proceeded on my original vow to try anything to mitigate my condition.

Why not just take the medication and be happy? For one thing, it's a powerful steroid—prednisone—that carries significant side effects. Long-term users experience weight gain, anxiety, flushing, vision blurring, and a whole host of other troubles. Worse, it weakens your immune system, the complex and marvelous biochemical mechanism your body has to fend off disease by itself. I don't want to make myself sick by popping pills. Over a course of years, steroid use often proves the old saying that the cure is worse than the disease.

So I undertook a series of steps that are often considered part of holistic medicine.

I read up on inflammatory joint disease, and changed my diet radically—no red meat, no dairy products, no coffee (yikes), no alcohol, no simple carbohydrates. I consumed piles of steamed vegetables, turkey, beans and oatmeal. I traded coffee for herbal tea—rooibos, which is actually quite good and has long been prescribed for anti-inflammatory use.

I started weekly visits to a physical therapist, who works with whatever joint is troubling me that week—my left shoulder, say—or guides me in use of a "reformer," a Pilates machine. I regularly avail myself of massage therapy; I've even been to Rolfing.

I adopted yoga in a big way, taking therapeutic yoga classes (called viniyoga) twice a week and incorporating a 40-minute routine into my life every day.

My sister, a psychiatrist, advised me to reduce stress by scaling back significantly my role at The Neenan Company. I sold controlling interest to my longtime partner, Randy Myers; he's now president, I'm the chairman, I work for Randy and everything is going well for The Neenan Company, Randy and me. I have issued my last "command" to a Neenan employee; henceforth, I direct feedback to Randy. He passes it on as he feels best.

My goal was to reduce my use of prednisone to the point I could take an absolute minimum dose, which became the case in early 2011. I also keep up with physical therapy, yoga, diet modification (though not as stringent as at the start) and stress reduction. I'm back on my bike, riding 15 miles at a time, moderately. No hundred-mile rides, maybe none ever again.

What caused my polymyalgia? I have no idea. I had been taking Lipitor, which may have been the culprit. It could have been stress, age, whatever. It's irrelevant, because for chronic disease, identifying the cause is a matter of intellectual curiosity more than practical action. It's how you respond to what has happened that matters. There is no such thing as a magic bullet, but many people delude themselves into thinking that if they can identify the precise cause of trouble, they can blot it out (or just take the right pill) and skip merrily along the primrose path evermore.

What I learned is what I have always known—the more responsibility I take for my own life, the better the result and the happier I am. I believe that as we grow older we have a moral obligation to be happy, to avoid going around and slapping people in the face with our negativity. That includes taking responsibility for whatever might be making us feel negative in the first place. Hard to be cheerful when you're hurting.

Now I can get on—and off—my bike. I've earned that, and I've earned my general wellbeing. Emerson said the first wealth is health. We must earn both, and when we do it's marvelous.

Chapter 22

Meaning: Only you can answer the big Why

Tell the truth, work hard, and come to dinner on time.
—Gerald R. Ford

Life is the sum of all your choices. —Albert Camus

I wanted to become a "wise elder."

I'd led The Neenan Company to consistent success as a design-build contractor. We were nearing a quarter-billion dollars a year in sales; we had dozens of projects across our home state of Colorado, employed more than three hundred people, and had moved into brand-new headquarters. Sharon and I had bought the condominium near San Diego and were spending time in California, where two of our daughters had settled. It was time to turn the company over to successors and find a new path in life.

I was fifty-eight and still had lots of energy. I figured I'd present "Business & You" a half-dozen times a year in Europe, North America, and Asia. I'd be sought throughout the construction industry to explain how the industry could transform and redeem itself in the twenty-first century. It was an episode of spiritual yearning. My new path was destiny.

That's what I thought.

None of it worked.

I found myself restless. I began transferring control of the company through an employee stock ownership plan, turned my office over to my successor, and committed to spend at least a week each month in California. Then the dot-com bust deflated our business in early 2001, and 9/11 made things worse six months later. The Neenan Company started to lose money for the first time in fifteen years. We were forced to undertake two waves of layoffs. Morale fell, overhead rose, and project problems cropped up. I still had control of the company's stock, and I was unable to just let it be.

I had tried for years to separate my personal identity from the company I had run for so long, that carried my family name, at which I had faced so many challenges and learned so much. I tried Zen, meditation, sheer will. I still had a dream of trying to change the construction industry. And now the venue for all that was failing.

Could I have liquidated the company? Sure, I could have. But—

Liquidation is erasure, and I have long wanted to create something that would outlast me. So, in early 2004, I bought myself a ticket to Kansas City, wrote a letter in my head to my uncle Jimmy, rented a car, and drove to his grave. I sat down and described to him what was happening. I heard a voice: David, I told you years ago you couldn't turn the company over to just anyone.

I knew what that meant. I decided to return to The Neenan Company and try to lead it back to financial health. I was too young to be a wise elder. I was at the grave of a wise elder.

I call this process "visiting the ancestors." It's something followers of the Buddhist, Taoist, and Confucian traditions consider an ordinary and desirable part of life, as do Native Americans. Most students of leadership have heard the story of Lois, a woman on a bleak, alcohol-wracked reservation who went every Tuesday night to a local community hall, set up a circle of chairs and sat there by herself for two hours holding an AA meeting. Asked why she would do that all alone, she replied: "I wasn't alone. I was there with the spirits and the ancestors; and one day, our people will come."

In mainstream American society such activities are considered a little oddball. I'm indifferent, though, to social convention. "David," a friend of mine once told me, "I don't know if you're a visionary or crazy." I guess there's some of both. I enjoy creating environments in which people are challenged, and that includes myself. Although Camus charged that man is the only creature that refuses to be what he is, I do try.

Remember when I visited my dad's grave back in 1980? Let's be fashionable and "deconstruct" these graveside episodes. Obviously they are occasions to take stock of myself and my life at moments when a turning point is near. It clarifies my own thinking and feeling. But there's more to it than that.

Who was I talking to at my dad's and my uncle Jimmy's graves? Who was talking to me? The best answer I can give is, whatever power in the universe helps us find purpose and meaning in life. Notice I said "helps." Our part is the biggest piece. Realizing that I carry on the qualities, hopes, and dreams of those who have gone before me has been incredibly powerful in my life. We all have ancestors; the human race is an ongoing story of struggle and hope and doubt and faith. I visit the ancestors to bathe my soul in that never-ending stream.

The story of modern life is largely a search for meaning. The human race does not, as a whole, face any longer the threat of famine or widespread disease. So why are we here? Life is a miracle, but for what purpose? Why should we get up in the morning? The most compelling works of the past century, from Albert Camus to Gustav Mahler to John Steinbeck, try to answer this question. It's the key issue of philosophy, including the recent version I find most useful, existentialism.

The miracle of life became even more precious and evanescent to me in 2006 when a false positive on a routine cardiac test led me to believe, for a while, that I was in significant danger. Maybe death was imminent; I wanted to talk about it, but no one else did. For a month the puzzle deepened, until further tests showed I was fine.

But what meaning shall I take from that? Close brushes with death, real or not, are often cited as moments in which human beings reassess and re-evaluate their paths. My experience helped me reaffirm something I've known for quite a while, maybe the most significant of all the lessons I've learned: Meaning in life is something we create ourselves. Philosopher Peter Koestenbaum, one of my intellectual mentors, says that freedom and accountability are ours as facts of existence. We experience anxiety, guilt, fear, death, and evil because they are aspects of this freedom. The choices we make bring that freedom to life—give it meaning.

Choices is the key word. Thoughts do not bring meaning. Words are intellectually interesting, but they are not meaning.

Action is the doorway. You cannot find meaning while lying on the couch. Do we jump on a horse and head into new country? Go to sleep in a hay wagon creaking along? Put down a holdfast and stay put? As E. E. Cummings put it, "Unbeing dead is not being alive."

I've always placed responsibility near the top of my list of values. If I'm not responsible for my life, who is? Yes, events come our way unbidden, but we can choose our response. Remember Viktor Frankl, who survived Nazi concentration camps and concluded that the last freedom anyone can exercise, no matter what the circumstance, no matter how much has been taken away, is the freedom to choose our own attitude.

The touchstones of my life are integrity, persistence, passion, responsibility, humor, and vision; being a good husband, father, and provider; daring to be different. All these are also promises to myself about how I intend to live, and making and keeping promises about my future is the essence of responsibility.

I sit down at the end of each year and conduct an audit of myself. How did I do on my values, my principles, my goals? Then, I set a new year's agenda of goals. I find that simply making a list generates movement toward whatever I put on that list.

After all the achievements that made him one of the great leaders of humankind, Thomas Jefferson said that, as much as anything, he was proud of his early work as a nailmaker. Back then nails were costlier and more precious than they are now. Hand-forged, they were so valuable that pioneers heading westward would often burn down their sheds in order to retrieve the nails and take them along. Jefferson had made thousands of those nails. His handiwork literally helped bind together the homesteads of American hope.

I see that story as a metaphor for what means most to me in my life. In my family, my business, the network of learning I have been part of, the bonds and connections are the most valuable. Being part of these is a majestic source of fun and enjoyment, but it's clear to me that happiness does not bring meaning.

It's the other way around. Frankl's experience in the Nazi death camps led him to conclude that meaning derives from good works and deeds, triumph over adversity, and love. Notice how precise and simple his prescription is: "What matters ... is not the meaning of life in general but rather the specific meaning of a person's life at a given moment." He added, paraphrasing Nietzsche: "Those who have a *why* to live can bear with almost any *how*."

Notice how much Frankl's philosophy resembles my own about taking responsibility. Buoyed by that simple idea, Frankl was even able to take pleasure in small things—an extra crust of bread, a snatch of music. It was clear to him, as it is to me, that pleasures and enjoyments add flavor to life, brighten the color field of daily existence, yet are not the ground in which meaning takes root. I love the smell of coffee in the morning, the indulgent escape of reading thrillers, the breeze off the cornfields by which I ride my bike. These are cinnamon, nutmeg, and coriander for a daily dish whose substance is family life, work, and growth.

Frankl had ample opportunity to find meaning in work during his time at Matthausen, Theresienstadt, and Auschwitz. Inmates who worked survived, an ironic disposition of the cruel slogan emblazoned in wrought iron over the notorious Auschwitz gate, "Arbeit Macht Frei" (Work Makes Free). You can see the gate to this day at Auschwitz, a World Heritage site in southern Poland that's one of the most memorable places I have ever visited.

Frankl's compatriots who lagged were exterminated. Others who survived focused on helping their fellows, and Frankl himself gained strength and satisfaction from that, offering his expertise as a physician. Yet that's not where he truly found meaning. He thought instead of his family. At the very toughest moments—and who among us has ever faced anything as ghastly as a death camp?—Viktor Frankl simply pictured himself rejoining his wife after the war was over. He was taking responsibility for his future by making a promise to himself.

Although my financial affairs and self-image are closely tied to The Neenan Company, the company is much more than a financial vehicle. I view The Neenan Company as a means to supply something human beings need—facilities designed and built well (especially schools and health care clinics, which are our key specialties); to provide employees with work and income and the chance to create wealth; and to create a community of people who are living with integrity and conveying value to the world we inhabit. The reason I go to my office in the morning isn't to look at financial reports, though I do that. I go to work to take part in the never-ending story of human aspiration and endeavor.

If I were to describe my overall approach I'd call it exercising the pioneer spirit. It includes taking responsibility, finding and demonstrating passion, embracing love and other human beings, living as robustly as possible. I ask and treasure the love and support of other people—but I don't need or want handouts. People sometimes ask me what would happen if I lost everything (they mean, all the money). I'd get a job and soon enough, if nothing else, I'd be the manager at a McDonald's.

Love, passion, and responsibility: All these ideas are only abstractions until they're put to use. If you want love, practice it. If you want wealth, earn it. If you lack challenge, seek it out. If you meet adversity, face it. I know we all can do it. If you don't know this, I promise that once you have taken a stand in the face of uncertainty, you *will* know it. The universe is a limitless experience, and there are adventures out there for all human beings. Learn to dance, write a song, raise a child, start a business, hike up a mountain, run for office, volunteer your time, make an investment, sign a contract, plant a garden, learn to cook, take up skiing, travel to Tashkent.

The possibilities are infinite, but life is not. As Paul Bowles wrote in *The Sheltering Sky*:

"We get to think of life as an inexhaustible well. Yet everything happens only a certain number of times, and a very small number, really. How many more times will you remember a certain afternoon of your childhood, some afternoon that's so deeply a part of your being that you can't even conceive of your life without it? Perhaps four or five times more. Perhaps not even that. How many more times will you watch the full moon rise? Perhaps twenty. And yet it all seems limitless."

What is limitless is not life but our choices within it. Please, awaken your life. Strive and risk and love and fail, and do it all again. Taste and touch and sing and fall and fly—and do all that again, too. Again, and again, and again.

Real wealth is the simple richness of life. It's our birthright. We honor that gift by exercising responsibility. Therein lies the meaning in my life.

There is no excuse not to wrap our arms wholly around all of life, and dance. Say yes.

For Further Reading

A Whole New Mind; Daniel H. Pink. We get so busy with the parts, we forget the whole. We are all designers.

Change: Principles of Problem Formation & Problem Resolution; Watzlawick, Weahland, and Fisch. Investigating the unknown and questioning the known.

Conscious Business: How to Build Value Through Values; Fred Kofman. Finding your passion and expressing your values through work.

Critical Path; R. Buckminster Fuller. You don't belong to you, you belong to the universe.

Disclosing New Worlds; Charles Spinosa, Fernando Flores and Hubert L. Dreyfus. Rich, practical new interpretations of entrepreneurship in business and community.

Finite and Infinite Games; James P. Carse. Infinite players do not die at the end, but in the course of play.

Freedom & Accountability at Work; Peter Koestenbaum and Peter Block. Deep philosophic insight for the workplace.

How Real is Real? Paul Watzlawick. "It is the theory which decides what we can observe."

The Ecological Vision; Peter F. Drucker. Maintaining equilibrium between change and conservation.

Lateral Thinking; Edward DeBono. Creativity step by step.

Leadership on the Line: Staying Alive Through the Dangers of Leading; Ronald A. Heifetz and Marty Linsky. To lead is to live dangerously.

Man's Search for Meaning; Viktor E. Frankl. Frankl's astonishing discovery of hope and the will to live while he was at Auschwitz.

Mastery; George Leonard. How to attain mastery and fulfillment in our daily lives.

Minding the Body, Mending the Mind; Joan Brysenko. How to take control of your own physical and emotional well-being.

Out of the Crisis; W. Edwards Deming. Nothing happens without personal transformation.

The 5th Discipline; Peter Senge. How to build a learning organization.

The Adaptive Corporation; Alvin Toffler. Planning for the future in an uncertain world.

The Machine That Changed the World; James P. Womack, Daniel T. Jones and Daniel Roos. Revolutionizing Western industry with lean production.

The Mystery of Capital; Hernando de Soto. Why capitalism can triumph throughout the world.

The Origins of Virtue: Human Instincts and the Evolution of Cooperation; Matt Ridley. Man's most basic instinct—the desire for mutual aid and trust.

The Plague; Albert Camus. A powerful existential classic about finding meaning in the midst of struggle.

The Sheltering Sky; Paul Bowles. A stark and compelling depiction of the meaning and persistence of love.

The Structure of Scientific Revolutions; Thomas S. Kuhn. A landmark in the history of paradigms.

The Tree of Knowledge; Humberto Maturana & Francisco Varela. A clearly written guide to thought and perception.

The True Believer; Eric Hoffer. The dangers of zealotry, doctrine and mass movements.

About the Author

David Neenan is the founder and chairman of The Neenan Company, a nationally prominent design/build commercial construction company that employs more than 250 people and surpasses $150 million in sales. Neenan and his colleagues are the originators of Archistruction™, a design-build philosophy that blends many in-house professional disciplines to deliver high value to the client.

He is also the creator of the popular Business & You self-improvement workshops, which have reached thousands of people in more than a dozen countries. He has conducted in-house training for companies such as Hewlett-Packard, Remax, Walt Disney, Hilton Hotels and AT&T, and he is an executive in residence at the Colorado State University School of Business.

David lives in Fort Collins, Colorado, and Del Mar, California, and has traveled to more than 50 countries. David and his wife, Sharon, have raised four daughters; he is an avid bicyclist.

David met his coauthor, **Eric Lucas**, when David was president of the Fort Collins School Board and Eric was a reporter at the local newspaper. Eric now lives in Seattle, Washington, and is an international travel and business writer whose work appears in Michelin Travel Publications, MSN.com, *Westways* Magazine and many other outlets. Eric is also an organic garlic grower, and an avid skier and outdoorsman.

Printed in the USA
CPSIA information can be obtained
at www.ICGtesting.com
JSHW022140250324
59878JS00002B/154